Computer Crime, Abuse, Liability and Security

A Comprehensive Bibliography, 1970–1984

compiled by
Reba A. Best and D. Cheryn Picquet

McFarland & Company, Inc., Publishers
Jefferson, North Carolina, and London

Dedicated to the memory of John W. Best and
with gratitude to Margaret Cassell Picquet.

Library of Congress Cataloging in Publication Data

Best, Reba A.
Computer crime, abuse, liability, and security.

1. Computer crimes – United States – Bibliography.
2. Electronic data processing departments – Security – Bibliography.
I. Picquet, D. Cheryn.   II. Title.
Z5703.4.C63B47 1985 [HV6773.2]   016.3641′68   84-43210

ISBN 0-89950-148-6 (pbk. : alk. paper)

Printed in the United States of America

McFarland   Box 611   Jefferson NC 28640

Table of Contents

Acknowledgments

The authors gratefully acknowledge the assistance of
Cheryl L. Campbell, Gloria Sisson Bickers, and Jeannie Emantel
in the preparation of this manuscript.

Introduction

Bits, bytes, ROMs, RAMs, chips, CPUs, COBOL, BASIC—
like most sociotechnological trends, the computer age has
brought with it a language of its own consisting of old words
with new meanings, new words with no meanings to many of us,
and many, many acronyms.
In a similar manner but with greater significance, this
hi-tech age has introduced to society a new world of crime.
Data diddling, hacking, superzapping, logic bombs, salami techniques, piggybacking—computer-related crime and abuse have
also brought society a new lingo. More importantly, it has
engendered its own brand of crime and abuse and given a new
twist to old crimes. Theft, embezzlement, fraud, and larceny,
among other "traditional" crimes, have found a new modus
operandi and a new type of criminal in the computer or hi-tech
environment.
Computer crime has produced its own set of criminals
and the need for new security systems and techniques, new
investigation and detection methodology, and new trial techniques. Crime discovery has taken on new meaning, and the
world of evidence has undergone radical alterations.
In response to this hi-tech crime, federal and state gov-
ernments have created computer crime legislation or have incorporated such legislation into existing law. This law touches
upon multiple facets of most individuals' lives. Privacy, free-
dom of access to information, electronic fund transfers, credit
cards, and national security systems are targets of computer-
related crime and therefore of computer-related crime laws.
Other legal issues such as the patentability of software, data
processing protection, copyright, intellectual property and
proprietary rights, antitrust and trade regulation, transborder
data flow, illegal exports, and the purchase and sale of trade
secrets are further topics of computer crime and abuse legislation.
It is, therefore, the intention of the authors, through this
bibliography, to direct a divergent group of researchers in their

1

work regarding the varied and rapidly changing facets of computer crime, abuse, liability, and security.

A survey of the field of literature on computer crime and a study of the availability of relevant information have revealed the need for a bibliographic research tool in the technical, legal, and business fields. This work should meet that need.

Scope

The years since, and including, 1970 are covered. The 1970 date was chosen primarily because of the significance of the early 1970's in the history of computer-related crime. According to a 1979 report of the U.S. Department of Justice, computer abuse emerged as an issue in the 1940's. Other abuse was actually recorded in the 1950's, but no federally-prosecuted, computer-related crime was reported until late in the 1960's. In the early 1970's computer-related crime and abuse were burgeoning as were the field of computer technology and the common use of computers. Reseachers began to study the crime and abuse aspects of computer technology in 1971; and, in 1973, the first national conference on the topic was held and a resulting formal study was completed. It seems that 1970 is a chronological gateway to computer crime as a research topic.

The authors would consider the cut-off date of this bibliography to be mid-1984. Entries were added through the fall, but generally reflected titles published only through July or August, 1984.

Topic

Topical coverage includes literature on computer crime, abuse, liability, security, and other issues of direct relevance such as privacy, patents, copyright, and antitrust and trade regulation. As the index topics demonstrate, subject matter runs from the general to the specific—from law and legislation in general to the Semiconductor Chip Protection Act of 1984; from computer crime to hacking, embezzlement, or fraud; and from banks and banking to electronic fund transfers. Relative but separate issues, such as admissibility of computer-generated evidence, are included only if the discussion is based on direct relevance to a computer crime topic. To insure accessibility of materials cited, non-English language entries and local newspaper articles have been omitted.

Sources

Titles cited in this bibiography have been gleaned from the widest variety of sources available: computerized databases; legal, technical, business, and popular indexing; government publications (both agency and Congressional materials); and footnotes, citations, and bibliographies appearing in monographic treatises, series, and periodicals.

Through its design, scope, and coverage, this bibliography is intended to guide various types of researchers—student to professional—through their respective research projects. For the reader who is simply interested in a general view of legal aspects of the impact of computers on society, this bibliography should prove equally beneficial.

Format

This book contains four sections: a bibliography of books, a bibliography of articles, a coauthor index, and a subject index. The books and articles sections are individually arranged in alphabetical order by author name or by title for those publications listing no author. The entries are numbered continuously throughout these two sections.

The subject index contains approximately 200 terms by which both books and articles are indexed. Because books usually treat a wide array of topics within a general subject area, they are frequently indexed via the more general index terms.

The coauthor index is a listing of joint secondary authors of both books and articles. Access to these authors' works would not be possible without this index.

There exist, therefore, three means of access to this bibliography: by author through the alphabetical arrangements in the books and articles sections; by author through the coauthor index; and by subject through the subject index. A number of "see" and "see also" references appear throughout the subject index for the convenience of the user.

Bibliography – Books

1 Abrams, Marshall D., et al. **Tutorial on Computer Security and Integrity.** Long Beach, Calif.: IEEE Computer Society, 1977.

2 Adams, J. Mack, and Douglas H. Haden. **Social Effects of Computer Use and Misuse.** New York: Wiley, 1976.

3 **Advances in Computer Security Management.** (annual) Philadelphia: Heyden, 1980-.

4 American Bar Association. Section of Criminal Justice. Task Force on Computer Crime. **Comprehensive Federal Computer Crime Legislation – A Report.** Chicago: ABA, 1984.

5 American Institute of Certified Public Accountants. Auditing Electronic Funds Transfer Systems Task Force. **Audit Considerations in Electronic Funds Transfer Systems.** New York: The Institute, 1978.

6 Auer, Joseph, and Charles Edison Harris. **Computer Contract Negotiations.** New York: Van Nostrand Reinhold, 1981.

7 Bailey, F. Lee, and Henry B. Rothblatt. **Defending Business and White Collar Crimes: Federal and State.** 2nd ed. New York: The Lawyers Cooperative Pub. Co., 1984.

8 Baker, Richard H. **Scuttle the Computer Pirates: Software Protection Schemes.** Blue Ridge Summit, Pa.: Tab Books, 1984.

9 Baxter, William F., Paul H. Cootner, and Kenneth E. Scott. **Retail Banking in the Electronic Age: The Law and Eco-**

nomics of Electronic Funds Transfer. Montclair, N.J.: Allanheld, Osmun, Pub. Co., 1977.

10 Becker, Jay. The Investigation of Computer Crime. Seattle: Battelle Law and Justice Study Center, 1978.

11 _____. The Investigation of Computer Crime. Washington: U.S. Dept. of Justice, Law Enforcement Assistance Administration, 1980.

12 Becker, Robert S. The Data Processing Security Game: Safeguarding Against the Real Dangers of Computer Abuse. New York: Pergamon Press, 1977.

13 Bender, David. Computer Law: Evidence and Procedure. (looseleaf) New York: Matthew Bender, 1978-.

14 Bender, Mark G. EFTS, Electronic Funds Transfer Systems: Elements and Impact. Port Washington, N.Y.: Kennikat Press, 1975.

15 Bequai, August. Cashless Society—EFTS at the Crossroads. New York: Wiley, 1981.

16 _____. Computer Crime. Lexington, Mass.: Lexington Books, 1978.

17 _____. How to Prevent Computer Crime—A Guide for Managers. New York: Wiley, 1983.

18 _____. White Collar Crime: A 20th-Century Crisis. Lexington, Mass.: Lexington Books, 1978.

19 Bernacchi, Richard, and Gerald H. Larsen. Data Processing Contracts and the Law. Boston, Mass.: Little, Brown & Company, 1974.

20 Bigelow, Robert P., ed. Computers and the Law: An Introductory Handbook. 3rd ed. Washington, D.C.: Section of Science and Technology, American Bar Association; Chicago: Commerce Clearing House, 1981.

21 _____, and Susan H. Nycum. Your Computer and the Law. Englewood Cliffs, N.J.: Prentice-Hall, 1975.

22 Bing, Jon, and Knut S. Selmer. A Decade of Computers &

Law. Oslo, Norway: Universitetsforlaget, 1980.

23 Boorstyn, Neil, Hugh D. Finley and Peter I. Ostroff. **Protection of Computer Software.** Berkeley, Calif.: California Continuing Education of the Bar, 1983.

24 Brandon, Dick H., and Sidney Segelstein. **Data Processing Contracts: Structure, Contents, and Negotiation.** 2nd ed. Rev. by George Ian Brandon. New York: Van Nostrand Reinhold, 1984.

25 Branstad, Dennis K., ed. **Computer Security and the Data Encryption Standard: Proceedings of the Conference on Computer Security and the Data Encryption Standard Held at the National Bureau of Standards in Gaithersburg, Maryland, on February 15, 1977.** Washington: The National Bureau of Standards, 1978.

26 _____, and Clark R. Renninger, eds. **Government Looks at Privacy and Security in Computer Systems: A Summary of a Conference Held at the National Bureau of Standards, Gaithersburg, Maryland, November 19–20, 1973.** Washington: National Bureau of Standards, 1974.

27 Brooks, Daniel T., ed. **Computer Software Protection: A Pragmatic Approach: Proceedings of the Program, October 15–16, 1981, Dupont Plaza Hotel, Washington, D.C.** Springfield, Va.: Computer Law Association, 1982.

28 Brown, William F., ed. **AMR's Guide to Computer and Software Security.** New York: Advanced Management Research, 1971.

29 Browne, Peter S. **Computer Security Manual.** (looseleaf) Northboro, Mass.: The Computer Security Institute, 1983-.

30 Buffelan, Jean-Paul. **Computer Technology and the Right to Privacy: Judicial Computer Science.** Washington: World Peace Through Law Center, 1979.

31 Burch, John G., Jr., and Joseph L. Sardinas, Jr. **Computer Control and Audit: A Total Systems Approach.** Santa Barbara, Calif.: Wiley, 1978.

32 Burnham, David. **The Rise of the Computer State.** New York: Random House, 1983.

33 Bushkin, Arthur A. **A Framework for Computer Security.** Rev. ed. McLean, Va.: System Development Corporation; Springfield, Va.: (distributed) by National Technical Information Service, United States Dept. of Commerce, 1975.

34 _____, and Samuel I. Schaen. **The Privacy Act of 1974: A Reference Manual for Compliance.** McLean, Va.: System Development Corp., 1976.

35 Carroll, John Millar. **Computer Security.** Los Angeles: Security World Publishing Co., 1977.

36 _____. **Confidential Information Sources, Public & Private.** Los Angeles: Security World Publishing Co., 1975.

37 _____. **Data Base and Computer Systems Security.** Wellesley, Mass.: Q.E.D. Information Sciences, 1976.

38 Chamber of Commerce of the United States of America. **A Handbook on White Collar Crime: Everyone's Problem, Everyone's Loss.** Washington: The Chamber, 1974.

39 Clark, David D., and David D. Redell. **Protection of Information in Computer Systems: Tutorial.** New York: IEEE Computer Society, 1975.

40 Clinard, Marshall B., and Peter C. Yeager. **Corporate Crime.** New York: The Free Press, 1980.

41 Cole, Gerald D. **Design Alternatives for Computer Network Security.** Washington: National Bureau of Standards, 1978.

42 Colton, Kent W., et al. **Computer Crime: Electronic Fund Transfer Systems and Crime.** Washington: U.S. Dept. of Justice, Bureau of Justice Statistics, 1982.

43 Comer, Michael J., **Corporate Fraud.** London: McGraw-Hill Book Company (UK) Limited, 1977.

44 Comptroller General of the United States. **Computer-Related Crimes in Federal Programs: Report to the Congress.** Washington: United States General Accounting Office, 1976.

45 _____. **Managers Need to Provide Better Protection for Federal Automatic Data Processing Facilities, Multiagency: Report to the Congress.** Washington: U.S. General Accounting Office, 1976.

46 **Computer Abuse.** (Litigation Course Handbook Series, no. 77). New York: Practising Law Institute, 1975.

47 **Computer Abuse 1976.** (Litigation Course Handbook Series, no. 88). New York: Practising Law Institute, 1976.

48 **Computer Crime: Computer Security Techniques.** Washington: Bureau of Justice Statistics, U.S. Dept. of Justice, 1982.

49 **Computer Crime: Criminal Justice.** Washington: National Criminal Justice Information and Statistics Service, 1979.

50 **Computer Crime: Criminal Justice Resource Manual.** Washington: National Criminal Justice Information and Statistics Service, U.S. Dept. of Justice, 1979.

51 **Computer Crime: Electronic Fund Transfer Systems and Crime.** Washington: Bureau of Justice Statistics, U.S. Dept. of Justice, 1982.

52 **Computer Crime: Expert Witness Manual.** Washington: Bureau of Justice Statistics, U.S. Dept. of Justice, 1980.

53 **Computer Crime: Legislative Resource Manual.** Washington: Bureau of Justice Statistics, U.S. Dept. of Justice, 1980.

54 **The Computer Framework for Complex Litigation.** (Litigation Course Handbook Series, no. 81). New York: Practising Law Institute, 1976.

55 **Computer Law: ALI-ABA Course of Study Materials.** Philadelphia: American Law Institute-American Bar Association Committee on Continuing Professional Education, 1984.

56 **Computer Law Developments: 1982-1983.** Washington: Computer Law Reporter, 1984.

57 **Computer Law Institute.** (Patents, Copyright, Trademarks and Literary Property Course Handbook Series, no. 166). New York: Practising Law Institute, 1983.

58 **Computer Law, 1981: Acquiring Computer Goods and Services.** New York: Practising Law Institute, 1981.

59 **Computer Law, 1982: Acquiring Computer Goods and Services.** New York: Practising Law Institute, 1982.

60 **Computer Law: Purchasing, Leasing, and Licensing Hardware, Software, and Services.** New York: Practising Law Institute, 1980.

61 **Computer Litigation: Resolving Computer Related Disputes and Protecting Proprietary Rights.** (Litigation Course Handbook Series, no. 216). New York: Practising Law Institute, 1983.

62 **Computer Litigation 1984: Resolving Computer Related Disputes and Protecting Proprietary Rights.** (Litigation Course Handbook Series, no. 249). New York: Practising Law Institute, 1984.

63 **Computer Programs & Data Bases: Perfecting, Protecting & Licensing Proprietary Rights After the 1980 Copyright Amendments.** New York: Law & Business, Inc./Harcourt Brace Jovanovich, 1981.

64 **Computer Security and Privacy Symposium: Proceedings, April 6–7, 1976.** Waltham, Mass.: Honeywell Information Systems, 1976.

65 **Computer Security and Privacy Symposium: Proceedings, April 18–19, 1978.** Waltham, Mass.: Honeywell Information Systems, 1978.

66 **Computer Security and Privacy Symposium: Proceedings, April 15–16, 1980.** Waltham, Mass.: Honeywell Information Systems, 1980.

67 Computer Security Institute. **Computer Security Handbook: The Practitioner's "Bible"** (looseleaf). Northborough, Mass.: The Institute, 1984.

68 Computer Security Research Group. **Computer Security Handbook.** New York: Macmillan Information, 1973.

69 Computer Security Risk Analysis. Boca Raton, Fla.: Advent Group, 1983.

70 Computer Software 1984: Protection and Marketing. (Patents, Copyrights, Trademarks and Literary Property Course Handbook Series, nos. 183 and 184). New York: Practising Law Institute, 1984.

71 Computer Software Protection: A Pragmatic Approach: Proceedings of the Program, October 15-16, 1981, Washington, D.C. Springfield: The Computer Law Association, 1982.

72 Computers, Contracts & Law. Uxbridge, Eng.: Online, 1979.

73 Computers, Privacy and the Law. St. Paul: Advanced Legal Education, Hamline University School of Law, 1983.

74 Contesting Computer Disputes: Litigation & Other Remedies in Contract, Trade Secret and Copyright Cases. New York: Law and Business, Inc., 1981.

75 Curry, Jack Pritchard. **Computer Security and Privacy.** (thesis) Chico, Calif.: Pritchard, 1975.

76 David, Lanny J., Don A. Allen, et al. **A User's Guide to Computer Contracting: Forms, Techniques, Strategies.** New York: Law and Business, Inc./Harcourt Brace Jovanovich, 1984.

77 Department of Health, Education, and Welfare. Secretary's Advisory Committee on Automated Personal Data Systems. **Records, Computers, and the Rights of Citizens; A Report.** Cambridge, Mass.: MIT Press, 1973.

78 Dial, O.E., and Edward M. Goldberg. **Privacy, Security and Computers: Guidelines for Municipal and Other Public Information Systems.** New York: Praeger, 1975.

79 Dinardo, C.T. **Computers and Security.** (Information Technology Series, v. 3) Montvale, N.J.: AFIPS Press, 1978.

80 Dirks, Raymond L., and Leonard Gross. **The Great Wall Street Scandal.** New York: McGraw-Hill, 1974.

81 Domestic and International Business Administration. **Crime in Service Industries.** Washington: The Administration, 1977.

82 Donnelly, Denis, ed. **The Computer Culture: A Symposium to Explore the Computer's Impact on Society.** Cranbury, N.J.: Fairleigh Dickinson, 1984.

83 Doswell, R.T. **Word Processing: Security Guidelines.** Manchester, Eng.: NCC Publications, 1983.

84 **Electronic Fund Transfers.** (Commercial Law and Practice Course Handbook Series, no. 160) New York: Practising Law Institute, 1977.

85 **Electronic Fund Transfers: Current Legal Developments, 1981.** (Commercial Law and Practice Course Handbook Series, no. 257) New York: Practising Law Institute, 1981.

86 **Electronic Fund Transfers: Regulation E Compliance, 1980.** (Commercial Law and Practice Course Handbook Series, no. 230) New York: Practising Law Institute, 1980.

87 Ellis, Martin B. **The Electronic Fund Transfer Act and Federal Reserve Board Regulation E: A Compliance Guide for Financial Institutions.** Englewood Cliffs, N.J.: Prentice-Hall, 1983.

88 Enger, Norman L., and Paul W. Howerton. **Computer Security: A Management Audit Approach.** New York: AMACOM, 1980.

89 Epstein, Michael A. **Modern Intellectual Property.** New York: Law & Business/Harcourt Brace Jovanovich, 1984.

90 **Executive Guide to Computer Security.** Washington: U.S. Dept. of Commerce, National Bureau of Standards and Association for Computing Machinery, 1974.

91 Farr, M.A.L., B. Chadwick, and K.K. Wong. **Security for Computer Systems.** Manchester, Eng.: National Computing Centre, 1972.

92 Farr, Robert. **The Electronic Criminals.** New York: Mc-Graw-Hill, 1975.

93 Fenwick, William. **A Briefing on the Impact of Privacy Legislation.** Park Ridge, Ill.: Data Processing Management Association, 1975.

94 Fernandez, Eduardo B., Rita C. Summers, and Christopher Wood. **Database Security and Integrity.** Reading, Mass.: Addison-Wesley Publishing Co., Inc., 1981.

95 Flaherty, David H. **Privacy and Government Data Banks: An International Perspective.** London: Mansell, 1979.

96 _____. **Protecting Privacy in Two-Way Electronic Services.** White Plains, N.Y.: Knowledge Industry Publications, 1984.

97 Fong, Elizabeth. **A Data Base Management Approach to Privacy Act Compliance.** Washington: U.S. Dept. of Commerce, National Bureau of Standards, 1977.

98 Freed, Roy N. **Computers and Law—A Reference Work.** 5th ed., Rev. Boston: Freed, 1976.

99 Gara, Otto G., and Bruce A. Naegeli, eds. **Technological Changes and the Law: A Reader.** Buffalo, N.Y.: Hein, 1980.

100 Geis, Gilbert, and Ezra Stotland, eds. **White-Collar Crime: Theory and Research.** (Sage Criminal Justice System Annuals, v. 13) Beverly Hills: Sage Publications, 1980.

101 Gemignani, Michael. **Law and the Computer.** Boston, Mass.: CBI Publishing Co., 1981.

102 General Accounting Office. **Federal Information Systems Remain Highly Vulnerable to Fraudulent, Wasteful, Abusive, and Illegal Practices: Report.** Washington: GAC, 1982.

103 Gilchrist, Bruce, and Milton R. Wessel. **Government Regulation of the Computer Industry.** Montvale, N.J.: AFIPS Press, 1972.

104 Goode, Stephen. **The Right to Privacy.** New York: Franklin Watts, 1983.

105 Grapa, Enrique. **Comprehensive Security in Data Processing Systems: The State of the Art.** (thesis) Urbana: Dept. of Computer Science, University of Illinois at Urbana-Champaign, 1975.

106 Green, Gion, and Raymond C. Farber. **Introduction to Security.** Los Angeles: Security World Publishing Co., 1975.

107 Hamilton, Peter. **Computer Security.** London: Associated Business Programmes Ltd., 1972; Philadelphia: Auerbach Publishers, 1973.

108 Harris, Thorne D. **The Legal Guide to Computer Software Protection: A Practical Handbook on Copyrights, Trademarks, Publishing, and Trade Secrets.** Englewood Cliffs, N.J.: Prentice-Hall, Business and Professional Division, 1984.

109 Healy, Richard J., and Timothy J. Walsh. **Industrial Security Management: A Cost-Effective Approach.** New York: American Management Association, 1971.

110 Heineke, J.M. and Associates. **The Distribution of Illegal Incident Characteristics: Cases of Bank Fraud and Embezzlement, Computer-related Crime, and Insider Theft From Drug Manufacturers and Distributors.** Washington: U.S. Nuclear Regulatory Commission, 1980.

111 Heinrich, Frank. **The Network Security Center: A System Level Approach to Computer Network Security.** Washington: Dept. of Commerce, National Bureau of Standards, 1978.

112 Hellman, J.J. **Privacy and Information Systems: An Argument and an Implementation.** Santa Monica, Calif.: Rand Corporation, 1970.

113 Hemphill, Charles F., Jr., and John M. Hemphill. **Security Procedures for Computer Systems.** Homewood, Ill.: Dow Jones-Irwin, 1973.

114 _____, and Robert D. Hemphill. **Security Safeguards for the Computer.** New York: American Management Associations, 1979.

115 Henry, Nicholas. **Copyright, Information Technology, Public Policy.** New York: M. Dekker, 1975-1976.

116 Hoffman, Lance J., ed. **Computers and Privacy in the Next Decade: Proceedings of the Workshop on Computers and Privacy in the Next Decade, Asilomar Conference Grounds, Pacific Grove, California, 25-28 February, 1979.** New York: Academic Press, 1980.

117 _____. **Modern Methods for Computer Security and Privacy.** Englewood Cliffs, N.J.: Prentice-Hall, Inc., 1977.

118 _____, comp. **Security and Privacy in Computer Systems.** Los Angeles: Melville Pub. Co., 1973.

119 Hoffman, Paul S. **The Software Legal Book.** (looseleaf) Croton-on-Hudson, N.Y.: Shafer Books, 1984-.

120 Holmes, Grace W., and Craig H. Norville, eds. **The Law of Computers.** Ann Arbor, Mich.: Institute of Continuing Legal Education, 1971.

121 Hondius, Frits W. **Emerging Data Protection in Europe.** Amsterdam: North Holland Pub. Co.; New York: American Elsevier Pub. Co., 1975.

122 Hoyt, Douglas B. **Computer Security Handbook.** New York: Macmillan Information, 1973.

123 Hsiao, David K., Douglas S. Kerr, and Stuart E. Madnick. **Computer Security.** New York: Academic Press, 1979.

124 International Business Machines Corporation. **The Considerations of Data Security in a Computer Environment.** White Plains, N.Y.: IBM, 1970.

125 _____. **The Considerations of Physical Security in a Computer Environment.** White Plains, N.Y.: IBM, 1972.

126 _____. **Data Security and Data Processing.** White Plains, N.Y.: IBM, 1974.

127 _____. An Executive's Guide to Data Security: A Trans-
lation from an IBM Svenska AB Publication. White
Plains, N.Y.: IBM Corporation, 1975.

128 International Oslo Symposium on Data Banks and Society:
The Proceedings. Oslo, Norway: Universitetsforlaget,
1972.

129 Invited Papers on Privacy: Law, Ethics, and Technology,
Presented at the National Symposium on Personal Pri-
vacy and Information Technology, October 4-7, 1981.
Washington: American Bar Association, 1982.

130 Katzan, Harry, Jr. Computer Data Security. New York:
Van Nostrand Reinhold, 1973.

131 Keet, Ernest E. Preventing Piracy: A Business Guide to
Software Protection. Reading, Mass.: Addison-Wesley
Pub. Co., 1984.

132 Krauss, Leonard I. SAFE: Security Audit and Field Evaluation for Computer Facilities and Information Systems.
Rev. ed. New York: AMACOM, 1980.

133 _____, and Aileen MacGahan. Computer Fraud and
Countermeasures. Englewood Cliffs, N.J.: Prentice-
Hall, 1979.

134 Kuong, Javier F. Computer Auditing and Security Manual.
Wellesley Hills, Mass.: Management Advisory Publications, 1976.

135 _____. Computer Security, Auditing and Controls:
Checklists and Guidelines for Reviewing Computer Security and Installations. Wellesley Hills, Mass.: Management Advisory Publications, 1975-1976.

136 _____. Computer Security, Auditing and Controls:
Text and Readings. Wellesley Hills, Mass.: Management
Advisory Publications, 1974.

137 Land, John. Protection of Computer Software by Copyrights, Patents, and Trade Secrets. Los Angeles, Calif.:
Land, 1983.

138 Leepson, Marc. **Computer Crime.** Washington: Congressional Quarterly, 1977.

139 Leibholz, Stephen W., and Louis D. Wilson. **Users' Guide to Computer Crime: Its Commission, Detection and Prevention.** Radnor, Pa.: Chilton Book Co., 1974.

140 Lord, Kenniston W., Jr. **The Data Center Disaster Consultant.** 2nd ed. Wellesley, Mass.: Q.E.D. Information Sciences, 1981.

141 Lupton, William Lloyd. **A Study of Computer Based Data Security Techniques.** Monterrey, Calif.: Naval Postgraduate School, 1973.

142 Lyons, Norman R. **Understanding Computer Crime.** Sherman Oaks: Alfred Publishing Co., Inc., 1984.

143 McKnight, Gerald. **Computer Crime.** New York: Walker, 1974.

144 Madgwick, Donald, and Tony Smythe. **The Invasion of Privacy.** London, New York: Pitman, 1974.

145 Madnick, Stuart E. **Data Security and Data Processing.** Cambridge, Mass.: M.I.T. Center for Information Systems Research, 1975.

146 Mair, William C., Donald R. Wood, and Keagle W. Davis. **Computer Control and Audit.** 2nd ed., rev. & enl. Wellesley, Mass.: Institute of Internal Auditors, 1978.

147 Mandell, Steven L. **Computers, Data Processing and the Law: Text and Cases.** St. Paul: West Pub., 1984.

148 Marchand, Donald A. **The Politics of Privacy, Computers, and Criminal Justice Records: Controlling the Social Costs of Technological Change.** Arlington, Va.: Information Resources Press, 1980.

149 Martin, Claude R., Jr. **An Introduction to Electronic Funds Transfer Systems.** New York: Amacom, 1978.

150 Martin, James. **Security, Accuracy, and Privacy in Computer Systems.** Englewood Cliffs, N.J.: Prentice-Hall, 1973.

151 Miller, Arthur Raphael. **The Assault On Privacy: Computers, Data Banks, and Dossiers.** Ann Arbor: University
of Michigan Press, 1971.

152 National Bureau of Standards. **Computer Security Guidelines for Implementing the Privacy Act of 1974.** Washington: The Bureau, 1975.

153 _____. **Glossary for Computer Systems Security.** Washington: The Bureau, 1976.

154 _____. **Guidelines for Automatic Data Processing Physical Security and Risk Management: Category: ADP
Operations; Sub-Category: Computer Security.** Washington: U.S. Dept. of Commerce, National Bureau of
Standards, 1974.

155 _____. **Guidelines for Automatic Data Processing Risk
Analysis. Category: ADP Operations; Sub-Category:
Computer Security.** Washington: U.S. Dept. of Com-
merce, National Bureau of Standards, 1979.

156 National Commission on Electronic Fund Transfers. **EFT
and the Public Interest: A Report of the National Commission On Electronic Fund Transfers.** Washington:
NCEFT, 1977.

157 _____. **EFT In the United States: Policy Recommenda-
tions and the Public Interest: The Final Report of the
National Commission On Electronic Fund Transfers.**
Washington: The Commission, 1977.

158 National Commission on New Technological Uses of Copyrighted Works. **Final Report of the National Commission On New Technological Uses of Copyrighted Works.**
Washington: The Commission, 1978.

159 National Criminal Justice Information and Statistics Service. **Privacy and Security of Criminal History Information: Analyses of State Privacy Legislation, 1979 Supple-
ment.** Washington: National Criminal Justice Information and Statistics Service, 1979.

160 _____. **Privacy and Security of Criminal History Information: Compendium of State Legislation.** Washington:
The Service, 1978.

161 National Study Group on the Security of Computer-Based Systems. **Where Next for Computer Security? A Report.** Manchester, Eng.: NCC Publications, 1974.

162 Neumann, P.G., et al. **A Provably Secure Operating System: Final Report.** Menlo Park, Calif.: Stanford Research Institute, 1975.

163 Niblett, Bryan, ed. **Computer Science and the Law: Workshop Sponsored by the Science Research Council of the United Kingdom and the Scientific and Technical Research Committee of the EEC.** Cambridge, Eng., New York: Cambridge University Press, 1980.

164 _____. **Data Protection Act 1984: A Practical Guide.** London: Oyez Longman, 1984.

165 Niblett, G.B.F. **Digital Information and the Privacy Problem.** Paris: Organization for Economic Co-operation and Development, 1971.

166 Nicholas, Henry. **Copyright, Information Technology, Public Policy.** New York: M. Dekker, 1975–1976.

167 Norback, Craig T. **The Computer Invasion.** New York: Van Nostrand Reinhold Co., 1981.

168 Norman, Adrian R.D. **Computer Insecurity.** New York: Chapman and Hall, 1983.

169 Nycum, Susan H. **The Criminal Law Aspects of Computer Abuse: Applicability of the Federal Criminal Code to Computer Abuse.** Menlo Park, Calif.: Stanford Research Institute, 1976.

170 _____. **The Criminal Law Aspects of Computer Abuse: Applicability of the State Penal Laws to Computer Abuse.** Menlo Park, Calif.: Stanford Research Institute, 1976.

171 _____. **The Criminal Law Aspects of Computer Abuse: Applicability of the State Penal Laws to Computer Abuse: Appendix.** Menlo Park, Calif.: Stanford Research Institute, 1976.

172 _____. Criminal Sanctions Under the Privacy Act of
        1974. Menlo Park, Calif.: Stanford Research Institute,
        1976.

173 _____. Legal Protection of Proprietary Rights In Soft-
        ware. Menlo Park, Calif.: Stanford Research Institute,
        1976.

174 _____, and George H. Bosworth. Software Proprietary
        Rights: A Legal Guide. Reston, Va.: Reston Publishing
        Co., 1983.

175 The Ombudsman Committee on Privacy, Los Angeles Chap-
        ter. Privacy, Security, and the Information Processing
        Industry. New York: The Association for Computing
        Machinery, 1976.

176 Orceyre, Michel J., and Robert H. Courtney, Jr. Consider-
        ations in the Selection of Security Measures for Auto-
        matic Data Processing Systems: Contributed to the Fed-
        eral Information Processing Standards Task Group 15-
        Computer Systems Security. Washington: U.S. Dept. of
        Commerce, National Bureau of Standards, 1978.

177 Organisation for Economic Co-operation and Development.
        Policy Issues in Data Protection and Privacy: Concepts
        and Perspectives: Proceedings of the OECD Seminar
        24th to 26th June 1974. Paris: Organisation for Econom-
        ic Co-operation and Development. Washington: sold by
        OECD Publications Center, 1976.

178 Parker, Donn B. Computer Security Management. Reston,
        Va.: Reston Pub. Co., 1981.

179 _____. Crime by Computer. New York: Charles Scrib-
        ner's Sons, 1976.

180 _____. Ethical Conflicts in Computer Science and
        Technology. Menlo Park, Calif.: SRI International, 1979.

181 _____. Fighting Computer Crime. New York: Scribner,
        1983.

182 _____. Manager's Guide to Computer Security. Reston,
        Va.: Reston Pub. Co., 1981.

183 _____. **Threats to Computer Systems.** Livermore, Calif.: Lawrence Livermore Laboratory, 1973.

184 _____, and Susan H. Nycum. **Computer Abuse Assessment and Control Study: Final Report.** Menlo Park, Calif.: SRI International, 1979.

185 _____, _____, and S. Stephen Oüra. **Computer Abuse: Final Report.** Menlo Park, Calif.: Stanford Research Institute, 1973.

186 Patrick, Robert L. **AFIPS System Review Manual on Security.** Montvale, N.J.: American Federation of Information Processing Societies, Inc., 1975.

187 Penney, Norman, and Donald I. Baker. **The Law of Electronic Fund Transfer Systems.** Boston: Warren, Gorham & Lamont, 1980.

188 Perry, Lawrence, and Hugh Brett, eds. **The Legal Protection of Computer Software.** Oxford, Eng.: ESC Publishing, 1981.

189 Perry, William E. **Computer Control and Security: A Guide for Managers and Systems Analysts.** New York: Wiley, 1981.

190 _____. **Computer Crime: Prevention, Detection, and Investigation.** Port Jefferson Station, N.Y.: FTP Technical Library, 1983.

191 Pritchard, J.A.T. **Computer Security: Facts and Figures.** Manchester, Eng.: NCC Publications, 1979.

192 _____. **Computer Security: Security Software.** Manchester, Eng.: NCC Publications, 1980.

193 _____. **Risk Management in Action** (cover title: **Computer Security: Risk Management in Action**). Manchester, Eng.: NCC Publications, 1978.

194 _____. **Security in On-Line Systems.** Manchester, Eng.: NCC Publications, 1979.

195 **The Privacy Issue and Computer Data Security: And Re-**

lated Materials. Rev. Washington: Sutherland, Asbill & Brennan, 1977.

196 Privacy Protection Study Commission. **The Citizen As Taxpayer: Appendix 2 to The Report of the Privacy Protection Study Commission.** Washington: G.P.O., 1977.

197 _____. **Employment Records: Appendix 3 to The Report of the Privacy Protection Study Commission.** Washington: G.P.O., 1977.

198 _____. **Personal Privacy in an Information Society: The Report of the Privacy Protection Study Commission.** Washington: G.P.O., 1977.

199 _____. **The Privacy Act of 1974: An Assessment: Appendix 4 to The Report of the Privacy Protection Study Commission.** Washington: G.P.O., 1977.

200 _____. **Privacy Law in the States: Appendix 1 to The Report of the Privacy Protection Study Commission.** Washington: G.P.O., 1977.

201 _____. **Technology and Privacy: Appendix 5 to the Report of the Privacy Protection Study Commission.** Washington: G.P.O., 1977.

202 **Problems Associated with Computer Technology in Federal Programs and Private Industry Computer Abuses.** Washington: G.P.O., 1976.

203 **Protecting Trade Secrets, 1983.** New York: Practising Law Institute, 1983.

204 Raysman, Richard, and Peter Brown. **Computer Law: Drafting and Negotiating Forms and Agreements.** New York: Law Journal Seminars-Press, 1984.

205 Reed, Susan K., and Dennis K. Branstad, eds. **Controlled Accessibility Workshop Report.** Washington: U.S. Dept. of Commerce, National Bureau of Standards, 1974.

206 Remer, Daniel. **Legal Care for Your Software: A Step-by-Step Guide for Computer Software Writers.** Reading, Mass.: Addison-Wesley Pub. Co., 1982.

207 Renninger, Clark R., ed. **Approaches to Privacy and Security in Computer Systems; Proceedings of a Conference Held at the National Bureau of Standards, March 4–5, 1974.** Washington: National Bureau of Standards, 1974.

208 Reymont Associates. **EDP Physical Security: Checklist and Briefing.** Rye, N.Y.: Reymont Associates, 1981.

209 _____. **Protecting Personal Information in Computer Systems.** Rye, N.Y.: Reymont Associates, 1978.

210 Ruder, Brian, and J.D. Madden. **An Analysis of Computer Security Safeguards for Detecting and Preventing Intentional Computer Misuse.** Washington: U.S. Dept. of Commerce, National Bureau of Standards, 1978.

211 Ruthberg, Zella G., ed. **Computer Science & Technology: Audit and Evaluation of Computer Security.** Washington: GAC, 1977.

212 Saltman, Roy G. **Copyright in Computer Readable Works: Policy Impacts of Technological Change.** Washington: U.S. Dept. of Commerce, National Bureau of Standards, 1977.

213 Sanders, Donald H. **Computers and Management in a Changing Society.** New York: McGraw-Hill, 1974.

214 Sardinas, Joseph L., Jr. **Computer Security and the Auditor's Responsibility: A Dissertation Presented.** University Park, Pa.: Pennsylvania State University, Graduate School, Department of Accounting and Management Information Systems, 1975.

215 Schabeck, Timothy A. **Computer Crime Investigation Manual.** San Francisco, Calif.: Assets Protection, 1980.

216 Schell, Roger R. **Computer Security: The Achilles Heel of the Electronic Air Force?** Maxwell Air Force Base, Ala.: U.S. Air University. Air War College, 1978.

217 _____, and Paul A. Karger. **Security in Automatic Data Processing (ADP) Network Systems.** Hanscom, Mass.: Directorate of Computer Systems Engineering, Electronic Systems Division, 1976.

218 Scott, Michael D. **Computer Law.** (updated annually) New York: Wiley, 1984-.

219 Search Group. **Standards for Security and Privacy of Criminal Justice Information.** 2d ed. Sacramento, Calif.: The Group, 1978.

220 Seidler, Lee J., Frederick Andrews, and Marc J. Epstein, eds. **The Equity Funding Papers: The Anatomy of a Fraud.** Santa Barbara: Wiley, 1977.

221 **Selected Electronic Funds Transfer Issues: Privacy, Security, and Equity.** Washington: Congress of the U.S., Office of Technology Assessment, 1982.

222 Sharratt, J.R. **Data Control Guidelines.** Manchester, Eng.: NCC Publications, 1974.

223 Sherizen, Sanford. **How to Protect Your Computer.** New York: American Management Associations Extension Institute, 1984.

224 Sieghart, Paul. **Privacy and Computers.** London: Latimer New Dimensions, 1976.

225 Simons, G.L. **Privacy in the Computer Age.** Manchester, Eng.: NCC Publications, 1982.

226 Simpson, Alan, ed. **Computer Privacy: Where to and Why.** Purley, Eng.: Input Two-Nine, 1977.

227 Sizer, Richard, and Philip Newman. **The Data Protection Act: What It Says, What It Means, and How to Comply.** Aldershot, Hants, Eng.; Brookfield, Ver.: Gower, 1984.

228 Sloan, Irving J., ed. **Computers and the Law.** New York: Oceana, 1984.

229 Smith, L. **Architecture for Secure Computing Systems.** Redford, Mass.: Mitre Corp., 1975.

230 Smith, Robert Ellis, and Keith B. Snyder. **Compilation of State and Federal Privacy Laws.** (annual) Washington: Privacy Journal, 1977-.

231 Soble, Ronald L., and Robert E. Dallos. **The Impossible Dream: The Equity Funding Story, the Fraud of the Century.** New York: Putnam, 1975.

232 _____ and _____. **The Impossible Dream: The Equity Funding Story, the Fraud of the Century.** Updated ed. New York: New American Library, 1975.

233 **Software Protection and Marketing: Computer Programs and Data Bases, Video Games and Motion Pictures.** New York: Practising Law Institute, 1983.

234 Sokolik, Stanley Lewis. **Computer Crime: Its Setting and the Need for Deterrent Legislation.** Springfield, Ill.: Data Information Systems Commission, Illinois General Assembly, 1979.

235 Soma, John T. **The Computer Industry: An Economic-Legal Analysis of Its Technology and Growth.** Lexington, Mass.: Lexington Books, 1976.

236 _____. **Computer Technology and the Law.** Colorado Springs: McGraw-Hill, 1983.

237 Somers, Leigh Edward. **Economic Crimes: Investigative Principles and Techniques.** New York: Clark Boardman, 1984.

238 Squires, Tony. **Computer Security: The Personnel Aspect.** Manchester, Eng.: NCC Publications, 1980.

239 Talbot, J.R. **Management Guide to Computer Security.** New York: Wiley, 1981.

240 Tapper, Colin. **Computer Law.** 3rd ed. New York: Longman, Inc., 1983.

241 Task Force on Privacy and Computers. **Privacy and Computers: A Report of a Task Force Established Jointly by Dept. of Communications/Dept. of Justice.** Ottawa: Information Canada, 1972.

242 Thorsen, June-Elizabeth, ed. **Computer Security: Equipment, Personnel and Data.** Los Angeles: Security World Publishing Co., 1974.

243 Turn, Rein, ed. **Advances in Computer System Security.** Dedham, Mass.: Artech House, 1981.

244 _____. **Privacy and Security in Personal Information Databank Systems.** Santa Monica, Calif.: Rand, Corp., 1974.

245 _____. **Privacy Protection in Databanks: Principles and Costs.** Santa Monica, Calif.: Rand Corp., 1974.

246 _____. **Privacy Systems for Telecommunication Networks.** Santa Monica, Calif.: Rand Corp., 1974.

247 _____, ed. **Transborder Data Flows: Concerns in Privacy Protection and Free Flow of Information.** Arlington, Va.: American Federation of Information Processing Societies, 1979.

248 United States. Congress. House. Committee on Banking and Currency. Subcommittee on Bank Supervision and Insurance. **Electronic Funds Transfer System (EFTS): Failure of the U.S. National Bank of San Diego: Hearings...Ninety-Third Congress, First Session, November 26 and 27, 1973.** Washington: U.S. Gov. Printing Office, 1974.

249 _____. _____. _____. Committee on Government Operations. Legislation and National Security Subcommittee. **Social Security Administration's Management of Data Communications Contracts With Paradyne Corp.: Hearings...September 13, 1984, August 2, 1984.** 2 vols. Washington: G.P.O., 1984.

250 _____. _____. _____. _____. **Privacy and 1984: Public Opinions and Privacy Issues: Hearing Before a Subcommittee of the... April 4, 1984.** Washington: G.P.O., 1984.

251 _____. _____. _____. Committee on Science and Technology. Subcommittee on Transportation, Aviation, and Materials. **Computer and Communications Security and Privacy: Hearings...Ninety-Eighth Congress, First Session, September 26; October 17, 24, 1983.** Washington: G.P.O., 1984.

252 _____._____._____._____._____. Computer and Communications Security and Privacy: Report.
Washington: G.P.O., 1984.

253 _____._____._____. Committee on Small Business. Small Business Computer Crime Prevention Act:
Report [To Accompany H.R. 3075]. Washington: G.P.O.,
1983.

254 _____._____._____._____. Subcommittee on
Antitrust and Restraint of Trade Activities Affecting
Small Business. Small Business Computer Crime Pre-
vention Act, H.R. 3075: Hearing...Ninety-Eighth Con-
gress, First Session, Washington, D.C., July 14, 1983.
Washington: G.P.O., 1983.

255 _____._____._____. Committee on the Judiciary.
Semiconductor Chip Protection Act of 1984: Report [To
Accompany H.R. 5525]. Washington: G.P.O., 1984.

256 _____._____._____._____. Subcommittee on
Civil and Constitutional Rights. Computer Crime: Hearing...November 18, 1983. Washington: G.P.O., 1984.

257 _____._____._____._____._____. Federal
Computer Systems Protection Act: Hearing...Ninety-
Seventh Congress, Second Session, on H.R. 3970...Sep-
tember 23, 1982. Washington: G.P.O., 1984.

258 _____._____._____._____._____. The Uni-
ted States Secret Service and Its Use of the National
Crime Information Center: Hearings...February 9, 1983.
Washington: G.P.O., 1984.

259 _____._____._____._____. Subcommittee on
Courts, Civil Liberties and the Administration of Jus-
tice. Copyright Protection for Semiconductor Chips:
Hearings...Ninety-Eighth Congress, First Session, on
H.R. 1028...August 3 and December 1, 1983. Washington:
G.P.O., 1984.

260 _____._____._____._____. Subcommittee on
Crime. White Collar Crime: The Problem and the Federal Response. Washington: G.P.O., 1978.

261 United States. Congress. Senate. Committee on Banking,
    Housing, and Urban Affairs. **Enforcement of the Ex-
    port Control Enforcement Act: Hearing...Ninety-Eighth
    Congress, Second Session, April 2, 1984.** Washington:
    G.P.O., 1984.

262 _____.   _____.   _____.   _____. Subcommittee on
    Consumer Affairs. **Electronic Fund Transfer Consumer
    Protection Act: Hearings...Ninety-Fifth Congress, First
    Session, on S. 2065...October 3, 4, and 5, 1977.** Wash-
    ington: G.P.O., 1977.

263 _____.   _____.   _____.   _____. Subcommittee on
    Financial Institutions. **Electronic Funds Transfer Sys-
    tems: Hearings...Ninety-Fifth Congress, First Session,
    on Oversight on the Report of the National Commission
    on Electronic Fund Transfers Entitled "EFT and the
    Public Interest," March 21 and 22, 1977.** Washington,
    G.P.O., 1977.

264 _____.   _____.   _____. Committee on Government
    Operations. **Problems Associated with Computer Tech-
    nology in Federal Programs and Private Industry: Com-
    puter Abuses.** Washington: G.P.O., 1976.

265 _____.   _____.   _____.   _____. **Staff Study of
    Computer Security in Federal Programs.** Washington:
    G.P.O., 1977.

266 _____.   _____.   _____.   _____. Subcommittee on
    Oversight of Government Management. **Computer
    Matching: Taxpayer Records: Hearing...Ninety-Eighth
    Congress, Second Session, June 6, 1984.** Washington:
    G.P.O., 1984.

267 _____.   _____.   _____.   _____.   _____. **Computer
    Security in the Federal Government and the Private
    Sector: Hearings...Ninety-Eighth Congress, First Session,
    October 25 and 26, 1983.** Washington: G.P.O., 1983.

268 _____.   _____.   _____. Committee on Small Business.
    **S. 1920, Small Business Computer Crime Prevention
    Act: Hearing...Ninety-Eighth Congress, Second Session,
    On S. 1920, Small Business Computer Crime Prevention
    Act, March 7, 1984.** Washington: G.P.O., 1984.

269 _____._____._____. Committee on the Judiciary.
Subcommittee on Criminal Justice. **Computer Systems
Protection Act of 1979, S. 240: Hearing...Ninety-Sixth
Congress, Second Session, On S. 240, February 28, 1980.**
Washington: G.P.O., 1980.

270 _____._____._____._____. Subcommittee on
Criminal Laws and Procedures. **Federal Computer Systems Protection Act: Hearings...Ninety-Fifth Congress,
Second Session, On S. 1766, June 21 and 22, 1978.** Washington: G.P.O., 1979.

271 _____._____._____._____. Subcommittee on
Patents, Copyrights, and Trademarks. **The Semiconductor Chip Protection Act of 1983: Hearing...Ninety-Eighth
Congress, First Session, On S. 1201...May 19, 1983.** Washington: G.P.O., 1984.

272 United States. Congress. **Small Business Computer Security and Education Act of 1984.** (Public Law 98-362)
Washington: G.P.O., July 16, 1984.

273 United States. Department of Health, Education, and Welfare. Secretary's Advisory Committee on Automated
Personal Data Systems. **Records, Computers, and the
Rights of Citizens: A Report.** Washington: U.S. Dept.
of Health, Education, and Welfare, 1973.

274 Van Tassel, Dennie. **Computer Security Management.**
Englewood Cliffs, N.J.: Prentice-Hall, 1972.

275 Virginia Advisory Legislative Council. **Computer Privacy
and Security: Report of the Virginia Advisory Legislative Council, to the Governor and the General Assembly
of Virginia.** Richmond: Commonwealth of Virginia, Dept.
of Purchases and Supply, 1976.

276 Wagner, Charles R. **The CPA and Computer Fraud.** Lexington: Lexington Books, 1979.

277 Walker, Bruce J., and Ian F. Blake. **Computer Security
and Protection Structures.** Stroudsburg, Pa.: Dowden,
Hutchinson & Ross, 1977.

278 Wallace, Jonathan D. **Law & Computer Software.** Sherman Oaks, Calif.: Alfred Pub., 1984.

279 Ware, Willis H. **Computer Data Banks and Security Controls.** Santa Monica, Calif.: Rand Corp., 1970.

280 _____. **Computer Privacy and Computer Security.** Santa Monica, Calif.: Rand Corp., 1974.

281 _____. **Computer Security in Civil Government and Industry.** Santa Monica, Calif.: Rand Corp., 1979.

282 _____. **Computers and Personal Privacy.** Santa Monica, Calif.: Rand Corp., 1977.

283 Waring, L.P. **Management Handbook of Computer Security.** Manchester, Eng.: National Computing Centre, 1978.

284 Westin, Alan F. **Computers, Health Records, and Citizen Rights.** Washington: U.S. Dept. of Commerce, National Bureau of Standards, 1976.

285 _____. **Computers, Personnel Administration, and Citizen Rights.** (Computer Science and Technology). Washington: U.S. Dept. of Commerce, National Bureau of Standards, 1979.

286 _____, and Michael A. Baker. **Databanks in a Free Society: Computers, Record-Keeping, and Privacy; A Report.** New York: Quadrangle Books, 1972.

287 Whiteside, Thomas. **Computer Capers: Tales of Electronic Thievery, Embezzlement, and Fraud.** New York: Crowell, 1978; New York: New American Library, 1979.

288 Wilk, Charles K., ed. **Selected Foreign National Data Protection Laws and Bills.** Washington: U.S. Dept. of Commerce, Office of Telecommunications, 1978.

289 Winkler, Stanley, ed. **Computer Communications: Impacts and Implications: The First International Conference on Computer Communication, Washington, D.C., October 24-26, 1972.** New York: available from Association for Computing Machinery, 1972.

290 Wong, Kenneth Kiu. **Risk Analysis and Control: A Guide for DP Managers.** Manchester, Eng.: NCC Publications, 1977.

291 Wood, Helen M. **The Use of Passwords for Controlled Access to Computer Resources.** Washington: U.S. Dept. of Commerce, National Bureau of Standards, 1977.

292 Wood, Michael B. **Introducing Computer Security.** Manchester, Eng.: NCC Publications, 1982.

293 Wooldridge, Susan, Colin R. Corder, and Claude R. Johnson. **Security Standards for Data Processing.** New York: Wiley, 1973.

294 World Intellectual Property Organization. International Bureau. **Model Provisions on the Protection of Computer Software.** Geneva: WIPO, 1978.

295 Zimmer, Robert C., and Theresa A. Einhorn. **The Law of Electronic Funds Transfer** (looseleaf) Washington: Card Services, Inc., 1978-.

Bibliography — Articles

296 "ADAPSO Boosts Ribicoff DP Crime Bill." **Computer Decisions,** 10, no. 1 (Jan. 1978), p. 13.

297 "ADAPSO Files Brief in Apple Software Case." **Computerworld,** 16, no. 45 (8 Nov. 1982), p. 125.

298 Abell, Bruce. "A Technology Assessment: The Social Consequences of Far Less Cash and Checks." **Computers and People,** 26, no. 2 (Feb. 1977), p. 7-10.

299 Abramson, Harold I., and Jay Martin. "The Impact of the Federal EFT Act on Customer Contracts in New York State." **University of San Francisco Law Review,** 13, no. 2 (Winter 1979), pp. 467-83.

300 "The Acid Test for Data Security: Try to Rip Off Your Own System." **Infosystems,** 29, no. 1 (Jan. 1982), p. 64.

301 "Action Promised on Crime Bill." **Computerworld,** 16, no. 18 (3 May 1982), p. 9.

302 Adams, Donald L. "Computer Fraud Goes to the DOGS." **EDPACS,** 5, no. 7 (Jan. 1978), pp. 8-9.

303 "Addressing Computer Crime Legislation: Progress and Regress." **Computer/Law Journal,** 4, no. 1 (Summer 1983), pp. 195-206.

304 "Administration Sets Out Transborder Data Policy." **Computer Law and Tax Report,** 5, no. 8 (Mar. 1979), p. 6.

305 Albi, Frank J. "Foiling the Computer Criminal." **Banking,** 70, no. 5 (May 1978), pp. 67-70.

306 Alderman, T. "Computer Crime." **Journal of Systems Management,** 28, no. 9 (1977), pp. 32-35.

307 Alexander, Charles, Joseph Pilcher, and Paul A. Witteman. "The Wells Fargo Stickup." **Time,** 117, no. 7 (16 Feb. 1981), pp. 64-65.

308 _____, Michael Moritz, and Bruce van Voorst. "Crackdown on Computer Capers." **Time,** 119, no. 6 (8 Feb. 1982), pp. 60-61.

309 Alexander, Tom. "Waiting for the Great Computer Rip-Off." **Fortune,** 90, no. 1 (July 1974), pp. 143-46, 148, 150.

310 "Algorithm Patentability After Diamond v. Diehr." **Indiana Law Review,** 15, no. 3 (1982), pp. 713-32.

311 Allen, B.R. "Computer Fraud." **Financial Executive,** 39 (May 1971), pp. 38-42+.

312 _____. "Menace of Computer Fraud." **Office,** 90 (August 1979), p. 74+.

313 Allen, Brandt. "The Biggest Computer Frauds: Lessons for CPA's." **The Journal of Accountancy,** 143, no. 5 (May 1977), pp. 52-62.

314 _____. "Embezzler's Guide to the Computer." **Harvard Business Review,** 53, no. 4 (July-Aug. 1975), pp. 79-84.

315 Allen, Pat. "Electronic Banking: It Could Change Your Future." **State Government News,** 19, no. 5 (May 1976), pp. 2-9.

316 Alpern, David M., and Mary Lord. "Preventing 'War Games'." **Newsweek,** 102 (5 Sept. 1983), p. 48.

317 "Amendments 'Seriously Deficient'." **Computerworld,** 15, no. 29 (20 July 1981), pp. 11-12.

318 "American Courts Point Up Canadian Security Problem: Just Who Was Guilty?" **Computer Law and Tax Report,** 3, no. 11 (June 1977), pp. 4-5.

319 Amir, M. "Computer Embezzlement—Prevention and Control." **The Computer Bulletin,** 15, no. 11 (Nov. 1971), pp. 397-400.

320 "And I Must Warn You, That Anything You Say Will Be Taken Down and Used in Evidence..." **Data System,** (Jan. 1978), pp. 11-12.

321 Anderson, Gene S. "Computer Manipulation Robs Our Firms of Millions of Dollars a Year." **Management World,** 6, no. 7 (July 1977), pp. 7-8, 10.

322 "Annual Survey of Rhode Island Law. Topical Survey. XIII. Recent Statutes. A. Criminal Law. 2. Computer Crime." **Suffolk University Law Review,** 14, no. 3 (1980), pp. 833-4.

323 "An Anomaly in the Patent System: The Uncertain Status of Computer Software." **Rutgers Journal of Computers, Technology and the Law,** 8 (1981), pp. 273-303.

324 "Anticrime Coverage Spreads to Computers." **Business Week,** no. 2736 (26 Apr. 1982), pp. 40, 42.

325 "Apple 'Bytes' Back: Copyrightability of Computer Programs: Apple Computer, Inc. v. Franklin Computer Corp." **University of Bridgeport Law Review,** 5, no. 2 (1984), pp. 363-92.

326 "Apple Computer, Inc. v. Franklin Computer Corporation Puts the Byte Back into Copyright Protection for Computer Programs." **Golden Gate Law Review,** 14, no. 2 (Summer 1984), pp. 281-308.

327 Apselbaum, H.E. "Patenting the Computer Program: Problem Pending." **Bell Laboratories Record,** 51, no. 4 (Apr. 1973), p. 1.

328 "Are Computer Contents Subject to Copyright? Study Seeks Answer." **Commerce Today,** 5, no. 13 (31 Mar. 1975), p. 17.

329 "Are Computer Programs Ever Patentable? Did the Patent Office Win?" **Jurimetrics Journal,** 13, no. 4 (Summer 1973), pp. 248-54.

330 "Are Trade Secrets the Way of the Future?" **Computer Law and Tax Report,** 5, no. 11 (June 1979), pp. 2-3.

331 Armer, Paul. "Electronic Funds Transfer Systems and the Consumer." **Computers and People,** 25, no. 6 (June 1976), pp. 8-9, 19.

332 _____. "The Individual: His Privacy, Self Image, and
    Obsolescence." **Computers and People**, 24, no. 6 (June
    1975), pp. 18-23.

333 Arnow, Jack A. "Computer Fraud Can Be Avoided If Safe-
    guards Are Applied." **Insurance**, 74, no. 7 (July 1973),
    pp. 31, 39.

334 "Arrest and Credit Records: Can the Right of Privacy Sur-
    vive." **University of Florida Law Review**, 24 (1972), pp.
    681-700.

335 "Arthur Young Loses Appeal on Trade Theft Conviction."
    Computerworld, 16, no. 16 (19 Apr. 1982), p. 79.

336 Ashman, Allan. "Software Program Can Be Copyrighted."
    American Bar Association Journal, 69 (Nov. 1983), p.
    1750.

337 Asija, S. Pal. "Computer Program Patents and the First
    Patent for Software." **Computers and People**, 30 nos.
    9-10 (Sept.-Oct. 1981), pp. 7-10.

338 Atkins, Susan E. "Computer Crime: Detection, Prosecu-
    tion, Deterrence." **Computers and People**, 29, nos. 9-10
    (Sept.-Oct. 1980), p. 25.

339 Auburn, F.M. "The Preservation of Privacy Bill 1972."
    Jurimetrics Journal, 13, no. 2 (Winter 1972), pp. 115-17.

340 Auer, Joseph, and Charles Edison Harris. "Master Cont-
    tracts." **Computerworld**, 15, no. 47 (23 Nov. 1981), pp.
    ID 1-4.

341 Bach, Gabriel. "Law and Politics in Transborder Data
    Flow." **Law/Technology**, 14, no. 2 (2nd Quarter 1981),
    pp. 1-24.

342 Bacon, Donald C., and Orr Kelly. "Uncle Sam's Computer
    Has Got You." **U.S. News and World Report**, 84, no. 14
    (10 Apr. 1978), pp. 44-48.

343 Baldigo, Michael E. "Computer Abuse: Past Is Prologue."
    The Internal Auditor, 37, no. 2 (Apr. 1980), pp. 90-93.

344 Ball, Leslie. "Data in WP: Very Valuable—And Very Easy to Steal." **Computerworld**, 15, no. 39 (28 Sept. 1981), pp. SR 53, 56-57.

345 Ball, Leslie D. "Computer Crime." **Technology Review**, 85, no. 3 (Apr. 1982), pp. 21-30.

346 Bangsberg, P.T. "Special Hong Kong Police Fight Computer Crime." **Journal of Commerce**, 361 (24 Aug. 1984), Sec. A, p. 3, Col. 3.

347 "Banking on Privacy." **Time**, 110, no. 13 (26 Sept. 1977), p. 59.

348 Barna, Becky. "A New Threat to Multinationals." **Computer Decisions**, 10, no. 8 (Aug. 1978), pp. 34-38.

349 Bartimo, Jim. "Bostonians Protest Parking Fine Collection." **Computerworld**, 16, no. 11 (15 Mar. 1982), p. 6.

350 _____. "Consultant Profiles Typical Computer Felon." **Computerworld**, 17, no. 10 (7 Mar. 1983), p. 25.

351 _____. "Courts 'Century and Half Behind' DP Crime." **Computerworld**, 16, no. 22 (31 May 1982), p. 12.

352 _____. "DP Plot Pads Agency's Books by $24.5 Million." **Computerworld**, 16, no. 10 (8 Mar. 1982), pp. 1, 8.

353 _____. "DP-Related Crime Rate Swelling?" **Computerworld**, 17, no. 28 (11 July 1983), pp. 1, 14.

354 _____. "Experts Find 'War Games' Pure Hollywood." **Computerworld**, 17, no. 32 (8 Aug. 1983), p. 6.

355 _____. "FBI Seizes Gear of 15 Suspected DP Hackers." **Computerworld**, 17, no. 43 (24 Oct. 1983), p. 5.

356 _____. "Feds Cracking Down on High-Tech Smugglers." **Computerworld**, 16, no. 9 (1 Mar. 1982), p. 2.

357 _____. "Fla. DP Law Credited with Switch to Guilty Plea." **Computerworld**, 17, no. 17 (25 Apr. 1983), p. 19.

358 _____. "HHS Privacy Act Update on Way." **Computerworld**, 16, no. 19 (10 May 1982), p. 18.

359 _____. "Hackers Beware—Firms Can Go Into Your Files."
Computerworld, 17, no. 37 (12 Sept. 1983), p. 12.

360 _____. "Love and Death Figure in $155,000 DP Scam."
Computerworld, 16, no. 18 (3 May 1982), p. 20.

361 _____. "Machines 'Tame the Monster' for U.S. Agency."
Computerworld, 16, no. 19 (10 May 1982), p. 19.

362 _____. "Report Characterizes DP Crime Expert Witness."
Computerworld, 17, no. 30 (25 July 1983), pp. 13-14.

363 _____. "Reports of Computer Crime Rising in Japan."
Computerworld, 16, no. 19 (10 May 1982), p. 17.

364 _____. "Senator, Honeywell Employees Guilty of Fraud."
Computerworld, 16, no. 48 (29 Nov. 1982), p. 7.

365 _____. "Tenn. Senator Indicted in Honeywell Swindle."
Computerworld, 16, no. 30 (26 July 1982), p. 14.

366 _____. "Three-Step Plan Curbs Abuse in Aid Programs."
Computerworld, 16, no. 19 (10 May 1982), p. 18.

367 Bartolik, Peter. "Customs Unleashes Import Intercept Operation." Computerworld, 17, no. 38 (19 Sept. 1983), p. 29.

368 _____. "Duo Charged with Offering to Erase Criminal
Records." Computerworld, 17, no. 30 (25 July 1983), p. 17.

369 _____. "Execs Speculate on Future of Hackers." Computerworld, 17, no. 37 (12 Sept. 1983), p. 8.

370 _____. "Mass. Bill Would Protect Intangible Material."
Computerworld, 17, no. 39 (26 Sept. 1983), p. 105.

371 _____. "Seven Dismissed for Alleged System Misuse."
Computerworld, 17, no. 32 (8 Aug. 1983), p. 18.

372 _____. "Shipper Out on Bail in Export Case." Computerworld, 17, no. 43 (24 Oct. 1983), p. 94.

373 _____. "U.S. to Ask Prison Term for Man Guilty of Sending Components to Soviet Bloc." Computerworld, 17, no. 33 (15 Aug. 1983), p. 10.

374 Baskerville, Richard. "Micro Protection Involves Physical Security." **Computerworld,** 17, no. 48 (28 Nov. 1983), pp. SR18, 22.

375 Bates, Amy Pierson. "Copyright Protection for Firmware: An International View." **Hastings International and Comparative Law Review,** 4, no. 3 (Spring 1981), pp. 473-508.

376 Batt, Robert. "Copyright Bill for Semi Designs Gets GOP Boost." **Computerworld,** 17, no. 48 (28 Nov. 1983), p. 143.

377 _____. "DP Security on the Rise." **Computerworld,** 18, no. 5 (30 Jan. 1984), p. 14.

378 _____. "Exec: DP Industry Hampered in California." **Computerworld,** 15, no. 39 (28 Sept. 1981), p. 63.

379 _____. "Export Act Hearing Stresses Free Trade Flow." **Computerworld,** 16, no. 51 (20 Dec. 1982), p. 51.

380 _____. "Importance of Data Security Campaign Stressed." **Computerworld,** 17, no. 41 (10 Oct. 1983), p. 24.

381 _____. "Industry Advised Against Premature Legislation." **Computerworld,** 17, no. 17 (25 Apr. 1983), pp. 89, 92.

382 _____. "Lack of Computer Security Examined by Symposium." **Computerworld,** 17, no. 18 (2 May 1983), p. 16.

383 _____. "Silicon Valley Seen Beefing Up Security with Cooperative Effort." **Computerworld,** 17, no. 39 (26 Sept. 1983), pp. 101, 108.

384 _____. " 'Trusted DP Systems' Seen Vital to Net Security." **Computerworld,** 17, no. 19 (9 May 1983), p. 25.

385 _____. "U.S. Accuses Fairchild of Improper Testing." **Computerworld,** 15, no. 26 (29 June 1981), p. 67.

386 "Battle Against Software Piracy Begins." **New Scientist,** 92, no. 1273 (1 Oct. 1981), p. 24.

387 "Battling the Computer Pirates." **The New York Times,** 132 (5 Jan. 1981), pp. D1, D7.

388 Bauer-Mengelberg, Stefan. "Parker v. Flook: A Formula to Cause Alarm." **IDEA,** 21, no. 2 (Spring 1980), pp. 75-114.

389 Beaser, Lawrence J. "Computerized Criminal Justice Information Systems: A Recognition of Competing Interest. An Introduction." **Villanova Law Review,** 22, no. 6 (Oct. 1977), pp. 1172-81.

390 Becker, Jay. "Editor's Foreword." **Computer/Law Journal,** 2, no. 2 (Spring 1980), pp. xi-xiv.

391 _____. "Rifkin, a Documentary History." **Computer/Law Journal,** 2, no. 3 (Summer 1980), pp. 471-720.

392 _____. "The Trial of a Computer Crime." **Computer/Law Journal,** 2, no. 2 (Spring 1980), pp. 441-56.

393 Becker, Louise Giovane. "Computer Crime." **Congressional Research Service Review,** 4, no. 7 (1983), pp. 21-22.

394 Beeler, Jeffry. "Apple Employees Arrested for Theft." **Computerworld,** 16, no. 21 (24 May 1982), p. 2.

395 _____. "Arsonist Torches DP Site While Backup Down." **Computerworld,** 15, no. 36 (7 Sept. 1981), p. 13.

396 _____. "Bank of America, Merrill Lynch Hit by Scam." **Computerworld,** 16, no. 51 (20 Dec. 1982), p. 5.

397 _____. "Bankrupt Law Firm Files Suit Against Vendor." **Computerworld,** 17, no. 44 (31 Oct. 1983), p. 16.

398 _____. "Bank's Source Code Tapes Vanish." **Computerworld,** 17, no. 23 (6 June 1983), pp. 1, 4.

399 _____. "Brown's Staff Faces Charges." **Computerworld,** 15, no. 29 (20 July 1981), pp. 1, 10.

400 _____. "California Law Redefines High-Tech Thefts as Felonies." **Computerworld,** 15, no. 42 (19 Oct. 1981), p. 5.

401 _____. "California Thieves Swipe Chips Worth $2.7 Million." **Computerworld,** 15, no. 49 (7 Dec. 1981), p. 9.

402 _____. "Charges Dropped Against Two in IBM Trade-
Secrets Case." **Computerworld,** 17, no. 28 (11 July 1983),
p. 4.

403 _____. "Chip 'Sting' Operation Nets Four." **Computerworld,** 16, no. 22 (31 May 1982), p. 2.

404 _____. "DPer Draws Three Years for Bribery, Kickbacks."
Computerworld, 15, no. 32 (10 Aug. 1981), p. 2.

405 _____. "DPers Charged with Stealing CPU Time." **Computerworld,** 16, no. 30 (26 July 1982), p. 9.

406 _____. "Defendants Say IBM Trade Secrets Not Secret."
Computerworld, 16, no. 34 (23 Aug. 1982), p. 4.

407 _____. "Eight Enter Innocent Pleas in IBM Trade Secrets
Case." **Computerworld,** 16, no. 28 (12 July 1982), pp. 1-2.

408 _____. "Expert: Incompetence Biggest Security Threat."
Computerworld, 15, no. 46 (16 Nov. 1981), p. 32.

409 _____. "FBI Nabs Student in Software Theft." **Computerworld,** 17, no. 40 (3 Oct. 1983), p. 2.

410 _____. "Five Japanese 'Stung' in Buy of IBM Secrets for
$650,000." **Computerworld,** 16, no. 26 (28 June 1982),
pp. 1, 4.

411 _____. "Former Calma Employee Held in Memory Board
Theft Scheme." **Computerworld,** 15, no. 27 (6 July 1981),
p. 10.

412 _____. "Former Sheriff's Deputy Pulls Jail Term for 'Accessing' Ex-Employer's Data Center." **Computerworld,** 16,
no. 28 (12 July 1982), p. 2.

413 _____. "Gov. Brown Sees Bright Side to Bid to Steal IBM
Secrets." **Computerworld,** 16, no. 28 (12 July 1982), p. 63.

414 _____. "Grand Jury Indicts Hitachi, 14 Employees." **Computerworld,** 16, no. 27 (5 July 1982), p. 1, 6.

415 _____. "Hacking—Mark of Genius or Plain Theft?" **Computerworld,** 17, no. 37 (12 Sept. 1983), pp. 1, 8.

416 _____. "Hitachi Enters Guilty Plea in IBM Trade-Secrets

Theft." **Computerworld,** 17, no. 7 (14 Feb. 1983), pp. 1, 8.

417 (Beeler, Jeffry, cont.) "Hitachi Pleads Innocent, Hints at Defense." **Computerworld,** 16, no. 32 (9 Aug. 1982), p. 6.

418 _____. "IBM Asks Order Forcing Hitachi to Drop Suit." **Computerworld,** 17, no. 33 (15 Aug. 1983), p. 7.

419 _____. "IBM Dispute Claim That Data in Espionage Case Worthless." **Computerworld,** 16, no. 41 (11 Oct. 1982), p. 4.

420 _____. "IBM, Hitachi Settle Civil Suit Out of Court." **Computerworld,** 17, no. 42 (17 Oct. 1983), p. 7.

421 _____. "IBM Slaps Suit on Hitachi, National Semi, NAS." **Computerworld,** 16, no. 39 (27 Sept. 1982), p. 4.

422 _____. "IBM 'Sting' File Stays Open: Judge." **Computerworld,** 16, no. 37 (13 Sept. 1982), p. 2.

423 _____. "IBM Suing Former Employee for Tech Theft, Business Venture." **Computerworld,** 17, no. 22 (30 May 1983), pp. 67, 70.

424 _____. "Insiders Seen Posing Greater Threat to DP Security Than Outsiders." **Computerworld,** 17, no. 37 (12 Sept. 1983), pp. 11-12.

425 _____. "Issues for DP Chiefs: Legal Liability, Protection." **Computerworld,** 17, no. 35 (29 Aug. 1983), p. 14.

426 _____. "Issues for Vendors: Source Code, Copyrights." **Computerworld,** 17, no. 35 (29 Aug. 1983), p. 15.

427 _____. "Judge Dismisses All Charges Against Three in IBM Case." **Computerworld,** 16, no. 40 (4 Oct. 1982), p. 6.

428 _____. "Lawsuits Seen on the Rise with Systems Use." **Computerworld,** 17, no. 19 (9 May 1983), p. 27.

429 _____. "Legislation under Study to Bag Welfare Cheats." **Computerworld,** 17, no. 17 (25 Apr. 1983), p. 16.

430 _____. "Magnuson Co-Founder, Associates Cleared of Trade Secrets Theft." **Computerworld,** 17, no. 47 (21 Nov. 1984), p. 8.

431 _____. "Microdata Settles Suit Filed by Express X Users." **Computerworld,** 17, no. 22 (30 May 1983), p. 4.

432 _____. "Mitsubishi, Four Employees Indicted in IBM Secrets Case." **Computerworld,** 16, no. 30 (26 July 1982), pp. 1, 8.

433 _____. "Mitsubishi Pleads No Contest to Trade Secret Theft Charges." **Computerworld,** 17, no. 44 (31 Oct. 1983), p. 4.

434 _____. "Mitsubishi Workers Miss Court." **Computerworld,** 16, no. 35 (30 Aug. 1982), p. 2.

435 _____. "Oakland Controller Files Fake Flight Plans." **Computerworld,** 15, no. 25 (22 June 1981), p. 4.

436 _____. "Organizations Step up Internal Data Security Efforts." **Computerworld,** 17, no. 37 (12 Sept. 1983), p. 10.

437 _____. "'Phone Freak' Going to Jail for Two Schemes." **Computerworld,** 16, no. 26 (28 June 1982), p. 7.

438 _____. "Police Nab Chief Suspect in Monolithic Theft." **Computerworld,** 16, no. 23 (7 June 1982), p. 6.

439 _____. "Programmer/Analyst Loots Rehab Fund for $17,000 He Was Entrusted to Protect." **Computerworld,** 17, no. 19 (9 May 1983), p. 15.

440 _____. "Qantel Distributor Countersues User for Fraud." **Computerworld,** 16, no. 47 (22 Nov. 1982), p. 10.

441 _____. "Recent Security Breach at Stanford Has University Officials Worried." **Computerworld,** 16, no. 6 (8 Feb. 1982), p. 13.

442 _____. "Reports of 'Break-In' Technique Called 'Hype'." **Computerworld,** 16, no. 13 (29 Mar. 1982), p. 15.

443 _____. "Security Specialists Form Group." **Computerworld,** 15, no. 30 (27 July 1981), p. 23.

444 _____. "Special Investigative Unit Formed to Protect DP Industry's Secrets." **Computerworld,** 17, no. 14 (4 Apr. 1983), pp. 93, 98.

445 (Beeler, Jeffry, cont.) "Supplier, Two Execs Charged with Conspiracy in Theft." **Computerworld,** 16, no. 24 (14 June 1982), pp. 107, 115.

446 _____. "TRW Password Theft Refocuses Attention on Security." **Computerworld,** 18 (2 July 1984), p. 2.

447 _____. "Trade Secrets Thefts Vex Tech Investments: Cary." **Computerworld,** 16, no. 44 (1 Nov. 1982), pp. 71, 74.

448 _____. "U.S. Alleges Hitachi Devised Secret Code." **Computerworld,** 16, no. 49 (6 Dec. 1982), p. 5.

449 _____. "Warrants Issued for Nine Hitachi Employees." **Computerworld,** 16, no. 31 (2 Aug. 1982), p. 6.

450 _____. "Yoshida Pleads No Contest in IBM vs. Hitachi Case." **Computerworld,** 17, no. 21 (23 May 1983), p. 2.

451 _____. "Youths May Face Charges of Accessing Los Alamos CPU." **Computerworld,** 17, no. 34 (22 Aug. 1983), pp. 1, 8.

452 Bellord, Nicolas J. "Computers and the Law: Progress." **New Law Journal,** 127, no. 5827 (10 Nov. 1977), pp. 1091-93.

453 Bender, David. "Post-Adkins Trade Secret Protection of Software." **Rutgers Journal of Computers and the Law,** 1970, no. 1 (Spring 1970), pp. 5-37.

454 _____. "Trade Secret Protection of Software." **The George Washington Law Review,** 38, no. 5 (July 1970), pp. 909-57.

455 _____. "Trade Secret Software Protection." **APLA Quarterly Journal,** 5, no. 1 (1977), pp. 49-70.

456 _____. "Who 'Owns' Employee-Developed Programs." **Computer Law Service,** 2, §3-4, art. 2 (1970), pp. 1-3.

457 Benton, John B. "Electronic Funds Transfer: Pitfalls and Payoffs." **Harvard Business Review,** 55, no. 4 (July-Aug. 1977), pp. 16+.

458 Bequai, August. "A Bright Future for the DP Criminal?" **Computerworld,** 17, no. 19 (9 May 1983), p. 41.

459 _____. "The Cashless Society: An Analysis of the Threat of Crime and the Invasion of Privacy." **Journal of Contemporary Law**, 3, no. 1 (Winter 1976), pp. 47-60.

460 _____. "Crooks and Computers." **Trial**, 12, no. 8 (Aug. 1976), pp. 48-49.

461 _____. "The Impact of EFTS on Our Criminal Justice System." **The Federal Bar Journal**, 35, nos. 3-4 (Summer-Fall 1976), pp. 190-205.

462 _____. "Legal Liabilities Arising Out of EFTS: A Checklist." **Commercial Law Journal**, 89, no. 6 (June-July 1984), pp. 289-90.

463 _____. "The Problem of Crime in the Electronic Society." **Commercial Law Journal**, 83, no. 3 (Mar. 1978), pp. 139-44, 149.

464 _____. "A Survey of Fraud and Privacy Obstacles to the Development of an Electronic Funds Transfer System." **Catholic University Law Review**, 25, no. 4 (Summer 1976), pp. 766-800.

465 Berman, Alan. "Passwords Not Only Way to Protect Terminals." **Computerworld**, 16, no. 13 (29 Mar. 1982), pp. SR 17-18.

466 Bernard, Jules. "Some Antitrust Issues Raised by Large Electronic Funds Transfer Systems." **Catholic University Law Review**, 25, no. 4 (Summer 1976), pp. 749-65.

467 Best, P.J. "Unauthorized Remote Access in an On-Line Real-Time System." **Australian Accountant**, 45, no. 2 (Mar. 1975), pp. 106-108, 111.

468 Betts, Mitch. "DP Crime Bill Toughened; TRW Data Base Breach Triggers Legislative Action." **Computerworld**, 18 (2 July 1984), p. 1.

469 _____. "House OKs Computer Crime Bill; Compromise Pending; Enactment Possible in '84." **Computerworld**, 18 (30 July 1984), p. 1.

470 _____. "Justice Department Proposes Computer Crime Bill." **Computerworld**, 18 (20 Aug. 1984), p. 2.

471 "Beware: Hackers at Play." **Newsweek,** 102, no. 10 (5 Sept. 1983), pp. 42-46, 48.

472 "Beware of Modern-Day Bonnies and Clydes." **Computerworld,** 17, no. 24 (13 June 1983), p. 21.

473 "The Big Four and the Secret Seven." **Computer Law and Tax Report,** 5, no. 11 (June 1979), p. 4.

474 Bigelow, Robert. "Copyright in Computerized Data Bases." **Computer Law Service,** 3 §4-3, art. 3 (1977), pp. 1-12.

475 _____. "Legal Protection of Software: A Matter of Monumental Insignificance." **Computer Law Service,** 3, §4-1, art. 5 (1978), pp. 1-2.

476 _____. "Transborder Data Flow Barriers." **Jurimetrics Journal,** 20, no. 1 (Fall 1979), pp. 8-17.

477 Bigelow, Robert P. "Attorney for the Computer User." **American Bar Association Journal,** 63 (July 1977), pp. 954-58.

478 _____. "Computer Contract Checklist." **Computer Law Service,** 2, §3-2, art. 5 (1975), pp. 1-17.

479 _____. "Computer Crime Is a People Problem." **Infosystems,** 27, no. 7 (July 1980), p. 80.

480 _____. "Infosystems, the Law and Patents." **Jurimetrics Journal,** 13, no. 3 (Spring 1973), pp. 129-31.

481 _____. "Legal Aspects of Proprietary Software." **Computer Law Service,** 3, §4-1, art. 1 (1979), pp. 1-7.

482 _____. "Some Legal and Regulatory Problems of Multiple Access Computer Networks." **Jurimetrics Journal,** 11, no.2 (Dec. 1970), pp. 47-62.

483 _____. "Symposium: Computers in Law and Society." **Washington University Law Quarterly,** 1977 , no. 3 (Summer 1977), pp. 372-75.

484 _____. "The Privacy Act of 1974." **Computer Law Service,** 4, §5-2, art. 5 (1975), pp. 1-18.

485 _____. "Researching Computer Law." **The Practical Lawyer,** 20, no. 1 (Jan. 1974), pp. 71-78.

486 _____. "Why Don't People Use Some Common Sense?" **Infosystems,** 29, no. 7 (July 1982), p. 87.

487 "Biggest Problem for Head of FBI's Computer Crime Training? Budget Constraints." **Computerworld,** 16, no. 43 (25 Oct. 1982), pp. 15-16.

488 Bilyeu, Robert. "Needed: Common Security Technique." **Computerworld,** 16, no. 43 (25 Oct. 1982), pp. 53-54.

489 Bishop, Timothy S. "Legal Protection of Computer Programs in the United Kingdom." **Northwestern Journal of International Law and Business,** 5, no. 2 (Summer 1983), pp. 269-95.

490 Blakeney, Susan. "Mass. T/S Exposes $129 Million Welfare Fraud." **Computerworld,** 16, no. 38 (20 Sept. 1982), p. 21.

491 _____. "Software Copyright Rulings Lack Consistency: Specialist." **Computerworld,** 16, no. 41 (11 Oct. 1982), pp. 83, 86.

492 _____. "Software Developers Planting 'Booby Traps'." **Computerworld,** 16, no. 28 (12 July 1982), pp. 7-8.

493 Blish, Eugene A. "Computer Abuse: A Practical Use of the AICPA Guide." **EDPACS,** 6, no. 3 (Sept. 1978), pp. 6-12.

494 Bloom, Robert. "Catching the Computer Crook." **Infosystems,** 27, no. 7 (July 1980), pp. 30-31, 34-35.

495 BloomBecker, Jay. "And a Little Child Shall Lead Them." **Computerworld,** 17, no. 41 (10 Oct. 1983), p. 43.

496 _____. "Case of the Daytime Moonlighters: A Reason for Making Preemployment Contracts." **Computerworld,** 17, no. 20 (16 May 1983), pp. 84-85.

497 _____. "Lessons from Wells Fargo." **Computerworld,** 16, no. 27 (5 July 1982), pp. 19, 22-27, 30.

498 _____. "Limited Statutes Abet Unauthorized CPU Users." **Computerworld,** 16, no. 36 (6 Sept. 1982), pp. 45-46.

499 _____. "The Trial of a Computer Crime." **Jurimetrics Journal,** 21, no. 4 (Summer 1984), pp. 421-35.

500 Blumenthal, David A. "Supreme Court Sets Guidelines for Patentability of Computer Related Inventions—Diamond v. Diehr." **Journal of the Patent Office Society,** 63, no. 2 (Feb. 1981), pp. 117-22.

501 _____, and Bruce D. Riter. "Statutory or Nonstatutory?: An Analysis of the Patentability of Computer Related Inventions." **Journal of the Patent Office Society,** 62, no. 8 (Aug. 1980), pp. 454-520.

502 Blumenthal, Marcia. "Adapso Adopts Position Paper for Copyright Law Revisions to Protect Software Industry." **Computerworld,** 15, no. 47 (23 Nov. 1981), pp. 55, 58.

503 _____. "Bankruptcy Trustee Calls OPM 'Massive Fraud'." **Computerworld,** 15, no. 47 (23 Nov. 1981), p. 11.

504 _____. "Contract Procedures a Must." **Computerworld,** 15, no. 33 (17 Aug. 1981), p. 10.

505 _____. "Exec to Law Forum: Computer Litigation to Reflect Industry Structure Changes." **Computerworld,** 16, no. 43 (25 Oct. 1982), p. 90.

506 _____. "FBI 'Stings' Engineer Trying to Sell Formula." **Computerworld,** 16, no. 34 (23 Aug. 1982), p. 6.

507 _____. "IBM Secrets Case May Alter Face of U.S./Japanese Links." **Computerworld,** 16, no. 35 (30 Aug. 1982), pp. 69, 82.

508 _____. "Lloyd's Insures Against EFT Theft, Writes First Policy for Irving Trust." **Computerworld,** 16, no. 3 (18 Jan. 1982), p. 22.

509 _____. STC Still Mum About Trade Secrets." **Computerworld,** 16, no. 10 (8 Mar. 1982), pp. 77-78.

510 _____. "Users Warned of 'Trusting' Contract Vendors." **Computerworld,** 15, no. 33 (17 Aug. 1981), p. 10.

511 Bockelman, Melvin F. "Police Department's Computer Security Kept Under Surveillance." **Infosystems,** 22, no. 5 (May 1975), pp. 65-68.

512 "Booby Traps That Catch Deadbeats." **Business Week,** no. 2741 (31 May 1982), p. 64.

513 Boockholdt, J.L., and J.S. Horvitz. "Prosecution of Computer Crime." **Journal of Systems Management,** 29 no. 12 (December 1978), pp. 6-11.

514 Boorstyn, Neil. "Copyrights, Computers, and Confusion." **Journal of the Patent Office Society,** 63, no. 5 (May 1981), pp. 276-87.

515 _____, and Martin C. Fliesler. "Copyrights, Computers and Confusion." **California State Bar Journal,** 56, no. 4 (Apr. 1981), pp. 148-52.

516 Borrell, Jerry. "Information Legislation of the 96th Congress." **Computer/Law Journal,** 3 (Winter 1982), pp. 125-45.

517 Bouvard, and Bouvard. "Computerized Information and Effective Protection of Individual Rights." **Society** (September/October 1975), p. 62.

518 Boyer, Barry B. "Computerized Medical Records and the Right to Privacy: The Emerging Federal Response." **Buffalo Law Review,** 25, no. 1 (Fall 1975), pp. 37-118.

519 Brace, Paul. "Electronic Funds Transfer System: Legal Perspectives." **Osgoode Hall Law Journal,** 14, no. 3 (Dec. 1976), pp. 787-95.

520 Brandel, Roland E. "Electronic Fund Transfer: Commercial and Consumer Law Aspects." **Commercial Law Journal,** 82, no. 3 (Mar. 1977), pp. 78-85.

521 _____. "The Relationship of Federal to State Law in Electronic Fund Transfer and Consumer Credit Regulation." **University of San Francisco Law Review,** 13, no. 2 (Winter 1979), pp. 331-60.

522 _____, and Anne Geary. "Electronic Fund Transfers." **The Business Lawyer,** 36 (Apr. 1981), pp. 1219-36.

523 _____, and Zane O. Gresham. "Electronic Funds Transfer: The Role of the Federal Government." **Catholic University Law Review,** 25, no. 4 (Summer 1976), pp. 705-38.

524 Branscomb, Anne W. "Global Governance of Global Networks: A Survey of Transborder Data Flow in Transition." **Vanderbilt Law Review**, 36, no. 4 (May 1983), pp. 985-1043.

525 Breyer, Stephen. "The Uneasy Case for Copyright: A Study of Copyright in Books, Photocopies, and Computer Programs." **Harvard Law Review**, 84, no. 2 (Dec. 1970), pp. 281-351.

526 Brictson, Robert C. "Information Policy, Computers and Privacy." **University of West Los Angeles Law Review**, 2 (June 1970), pp. 74-81.

527 Bristol, James T., and Lawrence Felton. "Social, Legal, and Ethical Aspects of Privacy in Computerized Public Welfare Records in Texas." **Law and Computer Technology**, 8, no. 6 (Dec. 1975), pp. 118-32.

528 "British Propose Data Protection Act." **Computer Law and Tax Report**, 5, no. 6 (Jan. 1979), pp. 5-6.

529 Britton, Herchell. "The Serious Threat of White Collar Crime." **Vital Speeches of the Day**, 47, no. 16 (1 June 1981), pp. 485-88.

530 Broadman, Ellen. "Electronic Fund Transfer Act: Is the Consumer Protected?" **University of San Francisco Law Review**, 13, no. 2 (Winter 1979), pp. 245-72.

531 Brock, Gerald W. "FCC Decision Starts Decontrol." **Computerworld**, 15, no. 26 (29 June 1981), pp. SR8, 10.

532 Brody, Marilyn A. "Copyright Protection for Video Games, Computer Programs and Other Cybernetic Works." **COMM/ENT**, 5, no. 3 (Spring 1983), pp. 477-515.

533 Brooks, Daniel T. "Copyright Act Codifies Employment Agreements." **Computerworld**, 16, no. 50 (13 Dec. 1982), pp. 25-26.

534 Brosnahan, B.C. "The Law and Computers." **Auckland University Law Review**, 1, no. 3 (Oct. 1970), pp. 1-36.

535 Brown, Harry L. "Auditing Computer Systems." **Management Accounting**, 54, no. 3 (Sept. 1972), pp. 23-26.

536 Brown, Nander. "Check Security Before Going Mini: Brown."
Computerworld, 16, no. 30 (26 July 1982), pp. 63-64.

537 _____. "Control Procedures the Key to Security." **Computerworld**, 16, no. 31 (2 Aug. 1982), pp. 63-64.

538 _____. "Question of Auditability Paramount." **Computerworld**, 16, no. 32 (9 Aug. 1982), pp. 61, 64.

539 Brown, Peter, and Richard Raysman. "Pending Legislation on Computer Crime." **New York Law Journal**, 191, no. 89 (8 May 1984), p. 1, col. 1.

540 Budnitz, Mark. "Problems of Proof When There's a Computer Goof: Consumers versus ATMS." **Computer/Law Journal**, 2, no. 1 (Winter 1980), pp. 49-65.

541 Budnitz, Mark E. "The Impact of EFT Upon Consumers: Practical Problems Faced by Consumers." **University of San Francisco Law Review**, 13, no. 2 (Winter 1979), pp. 361-404.

542 Bull, Gillian. "Recent Attempts to Achieve a U.K. Information Policy." **Computer/Law Journal**, 3 (Winter 1982), pp. 147-66.

543 Bumke, D. "Computer Crime." **Saturday Evening Post**, 252 (January/February 1980), pp. 28+.

544 Bund, Melvin. "Security in an Electronic Data Processing Environment." **The CPA Journal**, 45, no. 2 (Feb. 1975), pp. 33-35.

545 Burgess, John. "Computer Crime: Peril of Progress." **Trial**, 17, no. 1 (Jan. 1981), p. 6.

546 Burkert, Herbert. "Institutions of Data Protection—An Attempt at a Functional Explanation of European National Protection Laws." **Computer/Law Journal**, 3 (Winter 1982), pp. 167-88.

547 Burnside, J.W.K. "The Legal Implications of Computers." **The Australian Law Journal**, 55, no. 2 (Feb. 1981), pp. 79-92.

548 "Bushkin Terms Protectionism 'Disastrous'." **Computerworld**, 16/17, nos. 52/1 (27 Dec. 1982/3 Jan. 1983), p. 63.

549 "Businessman Gets Brief Sentence for Illegal Exports."
Computerworld, 17, no. 38 (19 Sept. 1983), p. 29.

550 Butel, Jane. "Consumer Protection and Electronic Funds
Transfer." Computers and People, 27, no. 1 (Jan. 1978),
pp. 10-11, 21, 23.

551 Bybee, Douglas. "Some Tips for Negotiating DP Contracts."
Computerworld, 17, no. 37 (12 Sept. 1983), p. 91.

552 Byron, Christopher, and Paul A. Witteman. "Dropping By
to Keep His Hand In." Time, 117, no. 10 (9 Mar. 1981),
p. 64.

553 "CONTU Chooses Copyright; Calls for Congressional
Changes--A Special Report." Computer Law and Tax
Report, 4, no. 11 (June 1978), pp. 4-7.

554 "CONTU Issues Software Subcommittee Reports, Asks for
Comments--A Special Report." Computer Law and Tax
Report, 3, no. 12 (July 1977), pp. 4-5.

555 "CONTU's Final Report Favors Copyright for Programs
and Data Bases." Computer Law and Tax Report, 5, no.
2 (Sept. 1978), pp. 1-4.

556 "CRT Message System Thwarts Two Thieves." Savings and
Loan News, 99, no. 2 (Feb. 1978), pp. 82-83.

557 Caine, Burton. "Computers and the Right to Be Let Alone."
Villanova Law Review, 22, no. 6 (Oct. 1977), pp. 1181-90.

558 Cairns, James G., Jr. "EFT: Who Is Riding Shotgun." ABA
Banking Journal, 74, no. 1 (Jan. 1982), pp. 47, 49, 51-52.

559 Campagna, Donald C. "Privacy as an Issue for Criminal
Justice Information Systems Managers." The Police
Chief, 45, no. 3 (Mar. 1978), pp. 49-51.

560 "The Campaign to Protect Personal Privacy." Business
Week, no. 2357 (16 Nov. 1974), pp. 88, 90.

561 Campaigne, Howard, and Lance J. Hoffman. "Computer
Privacy and Security." Computers and Automation, 22,
no. 7 (July 1973), pp. 12-17.

562 Campbell, R. "Privacy and Security in Local Government Infosystems." **Infosystems,** 23 (December 1976), pp. 31+.

563 "Can a Computer Be an Author? Copyright Aspects of Artificial Intelligence." **COMM/ENT Law Journal,** 4 (Summer 1982), pp. 707-47.

564 "Can a Programming Error Create Criminal Liability?" **Computer Law and Tax Report,** 5, no. 11 (June 1979), pp. 1-2.

565 "Canada Adds to Privacy Laws." **Datamation,** 24, no. 11 (1 Nov. 1978), p. 73.

566 "Canadian Government Report Calls for Strict Transborder Controls." **Computer Law and Tax Report,** 6, no. 1 (Aug. 1979), p. 3.

567 Carey, Frank T. "On Safeguarding the Right of Privacy." **The New York Times,** 123 (15 June 1974), p. 31, col. 2.

568 Carlton, J.L. "Security and Computerized Systems." **Management Accounting,** 55, no. 8 (Feb. 1974), pp. 33-36.

569 Carnahan, William H. "High Court Snags Patentability of Computer Programs." **The Air Force Law Review,** 16, no. 2 (Summer 1974), pp. 23-32.

570 "Case of the Purloined Password." **The New York Times,** 130 (26 July 1981), p. F4.

571 "Cashless Society: Electronic Fund Transfers and Model Legislation for California." **University of San Francisco Law Review,** 13, no. 2 (Winter 1979), pp. 521-47.

572 "Catching Computer Crooks." **Popular Mechanics,** 161 (June 1984), pp. 63-65.

573 "Catching Government Cheaters." **Computer Law and Tax Report,** 4, no. 8 (Mar. 1978), p. 5.

574 Cerullo, Michael J. "Computer Knowledge and Expertise of Public Accountants." **National Public Accountant,** 22, no. 12 (1977), pp. 32-38.

575 Chambers, A. D. "Computer Fraud and Abuse." **The Computer Journal,** 21, no. 3 (Aug. 1978), pp. 194-98.

576 Chambers, Andrew D. "Computer Abuse and Its Control." **EDPACS,** 6, no. 6 (Dec. 1978), pp. 3-12.

577 Chandler, James P. "Computer Transactions: Potential Liability of Computer Users and Vendors." **Washington University Law Quarterly,** 1977, no. 3 (1977), pp. 405-43.

578 _____. "Computers and Case Law." **Rutgers Journal of Computers and the Law,** 3, no. 2 (1974), pp. 202-18.

579 _____. "Proprietary Protection of Computer Software." **University of Baltimore Law Review,** 11, no. 2 (Winter 1982), pp. 195-255.

580 Chartrand, Robert Lee, and Jane Bortnick. "State Legislatures and Information Technology." **Law and Computer Technology,** 11, no. 2 (2nd Quarter 1978), pp. 39-59.

581 Choney, Liliane. "Trade Secrets Thefts Prompting Tighter Controls." **Computerworld,** 17, no. 48 (28 Nov. 1983), pp. SR29-30.

582 Christo, Thomas K. "DP Contracts Don't Leave Users Defenseless." **Computerworld,** 17, no. 24 (13 June 1983), pp. 73-74.

583 Clausen, Dale W., William E. Spaulding, and Thomas R. Wotruba. "Content Analysis: An Approach to the Computer Software Protection Controversy." **American Business Law Journal,** 17, no. 2 (Summer 1979), pp. 175-92.

584 "Clearer Laws on DP Access Asked by FBI." **Computerworld,** 17, no. 43 (24 Oct. 1983), p. 4.

585 "Coalition to Combat Software Piracy Forms in U.K." **Electronic News,** 30 (9 July 1984), sec. 1, p. 56, col. 1.

586 Coates, Joseph F. "The Future of Computer Data Security." **Vital Speeches of the Day,** 48, no. 9 (15 Feb. 1982), pp. 280-4.

587 Cohen, Gary M. "Computer Programs—Does the Law Provide an Adequate Protective Mechanism?" **The Australian Law Journal,** 56, no. 5 (May 1982), pp. 219-33.

588 Coiner, Lewis M. "Controlled Access System Uses Mag Cards to Restrict Entry for Tight Security." **Administrative Management**, 33, no. 12 (Dec. 1972), p. 14.

589 "Compaq Countersuit Claims Unfair Competition by TI." **Computerworld**, 17, no. 15 (11 Apr. 1983), p. 107.

590 "Computer Abuse Conviction Affirmed." **Computer Law and Tax Report**, 5, no. 8 (Mar. 1979), pp. 1-3.

591 "Computer Abuse: The Emerging Crime and the Need for Legislation." **Fordham Urban Law Journal**, 12, no. 1 (1983-84), pp. 73-101.

592 "Computer Canutes." **Solicitors' Journal**, 128, no. 34 (24 Aug. 1984), p. 569.

593 "Computer Capers." **Management Review**, 70 (April 1981), p. 6.

594 "Computer Capers." **Time**, 110, no. 6 (8 Aug. 1977), p. 53.

595 "Computer Cops and Robbers." **The Accountant**, 180, no. 5440 (3 May 1979), pp. 568-69.

596 "Computer Crackdown." **Fortune**, 110, no. 6 (17 Sept. 1984), pp. 141-42.

597 "Computer Crime." **American Criminal Law Review**, 18, no. 2 (Fall 1980), pp. 370-86.

598 "Computer Crime." **Editorial Research Reports**, 1, no. 1 (6 Jan. 1978), pp. 3-20.

599 "Computer Crime Can Add Up to Larger Losses." **Credit and Finance Management**, 82 (January 1980), p. 13.

600 "Computer Crime in Japan." **Computerworld**, 17, no. 45 (7 Nov. 1983), pp. ID7-ID8, ID17, ID20.

601 "Computer Crime Is a Well-Paid Profession." **Infosystems**, 26, no. 1 (Jan. 1979), p. 23.

602 "Computer Crime—Senate Bill S.240." **Memphis State Law Review**, 10 (Spring 1980), pp. 660-71.

603 "Computer Crime Skeletons." **Computerworld**, 16, no. 48 (29 Nov. 1982), p. 50.

604 "Computer Crime: The Danger Spreads." **Graphic Arts Magazine**, 53 (November 1981), pp. 98-99.

605 "Computer Crimebusters." **Black Enterprises**, 12, no. 10 (May 1982), pp. 59-60.

606 "Computer Criminals." **Intellect**, 106, no. 2390 (Nov. 1977), p. 187.

607 "Computer Criminals." **Science Digest**, 80, no. 2 (Aug. 1976), pp. 9-11.

608 "Computer Designers Building New Devices to Protect Data." **The Wall Street Journal**, 199, no. 89 (7 May 1982), p. 29.

609 "Computer Fraud." **Accountant**, 176 (February 10, 1977), pp. 167-8.

610 "Computer Fraud: A Power for Good and Evil." **The Banker**, 130, no. 649 (Mar. 1980), pp. 123+.

611 "Computer Fraud and Embezzlement." **EDP Analyzer**, 11, no. 9 (Sept. 1973), pp. 1-14.

612 "Computer Fraud Exaggerated." **Accountant**, 185 (27 Aug. 1981), p. 233.

613 "Computer Fraud: Growing Retail Menace." **Chain Store Executive**, 54 (June 1978), pp. 27-30.

614 "Computer Frauds Build Interest in Security." **Editor and Publisher**, 109 (29 May 1976), pp. 9+.

615 "Computer Group Urges Europe, U.S. Cooperation." **Computer Decisions**, 10, no. 2 (Feb. 1978), p. 6.

616 "Computer Literacy Threatens Data Secrecy." **The Economist**, 283, no. 7239 (29 May 1982), p. 93.

617 "Computer Matching Programs: A Threat to Privacy." **Columbia Journal of Law and Social Problems**, 15, no. 2 (1979), pp. 143-80.

618 "Computer Media Kidnappers Sentenced." **EDPACS,** 5, no.
     10 (Apr. 1978), pp. 16-17.

619 "Computer Privacy." **Scientific American,** 236, no. 2 (Feb.
     1977), p. 50.

620 "Computer Program Held Trade Secret." **Computer Law
     and Tax Report,** 5, no. 9 (Apr. 1979), pp. 4-5.

621 "Computer Program Patentability—The CCPA Refuses to
     Follow the Lead of the Supreme Court in Parker v.
     Flook." **North Carolina Law Review,** 58, no. 2 (Jan. 1980),
     pp. 319-58.

622 "Computer Program Protection in Three British Common-
     wealth Countries: What Can U.S. Learn?" **Idea,** 15, no. 2
     (Summer 1971), pp. 304-21.

623 "Computer Programs: Does the Copyright Law Apply?"
     Art and the Law, 5, no. 3 (1980), pp. 66-67.

624 "Computer-Related Fraud." **The CPA Journal,** 45, no. 6
     (June 1975), pp. 61-62.

625 "Computer Saboteurs." **Science Digest,** 92 (July 1984),
     pp. 58-61.

626 "Computer Security at HEW Below Standard, Study Finds."
     Computer Decisions, 10, no. 2 (Feb. 1978), p. 10.

627 "Computer Security: Backup and Recovery Methods." **EDP
     Analyzer,** 10, no. 1 (Jan. 1972), pp. 1-15.

628 "Computer Security Systems and Services." **Computer Sur-
     vey,** no. 6 (1977), pp. 2-6.

629 "Computer Security—The Imperative Nuisance." **Infosys-
     tems,** 21 (February 1974), pp. 24-28.

630 "Computer Software and Strict Products Liability." **San
     Diego Law Review,** 20, no. 2 (Mar. 1983), pp. 439-56.

631 "Computer Software: Beyond the Limits of Existing Pro-
     prietary Protection Policy." **Brooklyn Law Review,** 40,
     no. 1 (Summer 1973), pp. 116-46.

632 "The Computer Thieves." **Newsweek,** 81, no. 24 (18 June 1973), pp. 109-10, 112.

633 "Computerized Personal Information System Held Unconstitutional." **Computer Law and Tax Report,** 4, no. 6 (Jan. 1978), pp. 1-2.

634 "Computers and California Law—A Time for Decision." **Santa Clara Lawyer,** 11, no. 2 (Spring 1971), pp. 280-97.

635 "Computers and Criminals." **The New York Times,** 129 (27 Sept. 1979), p. D2.

636 "Computers in the Private Sector: Right to Informational Privacy for the Consumer." **Washburn Law Journal,** 22, no. 3 (1983), pp. 469-90.

637 "Computers, the Disclosure of Medical Information, and the Fair Credit Reporting Act." **Computer/Law Journal,** 3 (Summer 1982), pp. 619-39.

638 "Computing the Risks." **The Progressive,** 47 (Oct. 1983), pp. 11-12.

639 "Congress Blasts Poor Security: SSA Snafu Hit." **Computer Decisions,** 9 (April 1977), p. 8.

640 "Congress Gets Bill to Implement CONTU Recommendations on Program Copyrights." **Computer Law and Tax Report,** 6, no. 10 (May 1980), pp. 1-2.

641 "Congress Goes After Computer Crime." **Computer Law and Tax Report,** 4, no. 3 (Oct. 1977), pp. 1-3.

642 Conner, Richard L. "DP Lawyers and Litigation: Another View...Ways to Choose Prospective Attorneys." **Computerworld,** 17, no. 28 (11 July 1983), pp. 50-51, 53.

643 Conniff, Richard. "21st Century Crime-Stoppers." **Science Digest,** 90, no. 8 (Aug. 1982), pp. 60-65.

644 "Conning by Computer." **Newsweek,** 81, no. 17 (23 Apr. 1973), pp. 90, 93.

645 "Conspiracy Nets Gopal Jail Term." **Computerworld,** 15, no. 41 (12 Oct. 1981), p. 8.

646 "Constitutional Law—Right of Privacy—Drug Abuse Control—Whalen v. Roe." **New York Law School Law Review,** 24, no. 1 (1978), pp. 260-75.

647 "Contracting for Performance in the Procurement of Custom Computer Software." **Golden Gate University Law Review,** 13, no. 2 (Spring 1983), pp. 461-74.

648 "Controversial Driver Registry Bill Gets Thumbs Up from Congress." **Computerworld,** 16, no. 42 (18 Oct. 1982), p. 4.

649 "A Conversation with IBM's DeMaio—Commonsense Approach to DP Security." **Computerworld,** 18, no. 5 (30 Jan. 1984), pp. 15-16.

650 Coombe, George W., Jr., and Susan L. Kirk. "Privacy, Data Protection, and Transborder Data Flow: A Corporate Response to International Expectations." **The Business Lawyer,** 39, no. 1 (Nov. 1983), pp. 33-66.

651 Cooper, David M. "Transborder Data Flow and the Protection of Privacy: The Harmonization of Data Protection Law." **The Fletcher Forum,** 8, no. 2 (Summer 1984), pp. 335-52.

652 "Copyright: Computer Firmware: Is It Copyrightable?" **Oklahoma Law Review,** 36, no. 1 (Winter 1983), pp. 119-35.

653 "Copyright/Computer Programs." **Illinois Bar Journal,** 72, no. 9 (May 1984), pp. 486-91.

654 "Copyright for Integrated Circuit Designs: Will the 1976 Act Protect Against Chip Pirates?" **South Texas Law Journal,** 24, no. 3 (1983), pp. 817-50.

655 "Copyright in Computer Programs: A Hollow Victory." **The Modern Law Review,** 46, no. 2 (March 1983), pp. 231-35.

656 "Copyright Protection for Computer Programs in Read Only Memory Chips." **Hofstra Law Review,** 11, no. 1 (Fall 1982), pp. 329-70.

657 "Copyright Protection for Computer Programs under the 1976 Copyright Act." **Indiana Law Journal,** 52, no. 2 (Winter 1977), pp. 503-16.

658 "Copyright Protection for Programs Stored in Computer Chips: Competing with IBM and Apple." **Hamline Law Review,** 7, no. 1 (Jan. 1984), pp. 103–30.

659 "Copyright Protection of Computer Program Object Code." **Harvard Law Review,** 96, no. 7 (May 1983), pp. 1723–44.

660 "The Copyrightability of Object Code." **Notre Dame Law Review,** 59, no. 2 (1984), pp. 412–30.

661 "Copyrighting Object Code: Applying Old Legal Tools to New Technologies." **Computer/Law Journal,** 4, no. 2 Fall 1983), pp. 421–40.

662 "Copyrights and Intellectual Property—Visual and Aural Aspects of Video Games Are Properly Copyrightable Material." **Dickinson Law Review,** 87, no. 4 (Summer 1983), pp. 845–53.

663 Corasick, Margaret J., and Brian G. Brockway. "Protection of Computer-Based Information." **Albany Law Review,** 40, no. 1 (1975), pp. 113–53.

664 Corbett, James. "Computers and the Protection of Privacy." **New Law Journal,** 126, no. 5753 (3 June 1976), pp. 556–59.

665 Couch, Robert M. "A Suggested Legislative Approach to the Problem of Computer Crime." **Washington and Lee Law Review,** 38, no. 4 (Fall 1981), pp. 1173–94.

666 "Court Backs ROM Copyright." **Computerworld,** 15, no. 45 (9 Nov. 1981), p. 10.

667 "Court Reverses Alberta Conviction; Holds Computer Is Not a Telecommunication Facility; Nova Scotia Decides Otherwise." **Computer Law and Tax Report,** 6, no. 6 (Jan. 1980), pp. 1–3.

668 Courtney, Robert H., Jr. "Commonly Found Deficiencies in the Security of Data Processing Activities." **Computer Law Service,** 1, §2-2, art. 1 (1971), pp. 1–18.

669 _____. "Security Risk Assessment in Electronic Data Processing." **National Computer Conference,** 46 (1977), pp. 97–104.

670 "Crackdown on Computer Capers." **Time,** 119, no. 6 (8 Feb. 1982), pp. 60-61.

671 "Credit Bureaus Adopt Security Standards." **Computer Law and Tax Report,** 4, no. 4 (Nov. 1977), pp. 5-6.

672 "Crime by the Numbers." **Industrial Distribution,** 71, no. 11 (Nov. 1981), p. 46.

673 Criscuoli, E.J., Jr. "What Personnel Administrators Should Know About Computer Crime." **Personnel Administration,** 26 (September 1981), pp. 53-56.

674 Crisman, Thomas L. "Computer Program Protection. II. Patentability of Computer Programs." **Texas Bar Journal,** 34, no. 1 (Jan. 1971), pp. 33-35.

675 Cristiani, Katherine K. "The Electronic Fund Transfer Act: Some Compliance Problems for Banks." **University of San Francisco Law Review,** 13, no. 2 (Winter 1979), pp. 273-97.

676 "Crusade Against Computer Crime." **Credit Financial Management,** 84 (May 1982), p. 37.

677 "Cullinane Enhances 'Culprit,' 'EDP-Auditor'." **Computerworld,** 15, no. 45 (9 Nov. 1981), p. 85.

678 "The Current State of Computer Software Protection: A Survey and Bibliography of Copyright, Trade Secret, and Patent Alternatives." **Nova Law Journal,** 8, no. 1 (Fall 1983), pp. 107-43.

679 "DEC, COI Settle Patent Suit Out of Court." **Computerworld,** 15, no. 37 (14 Sept. 1981), p. 83.

680 "DG Guilty of Antitrust Violations." **Computerworld,** 15, no. 24 (15 June 1981), p. 2.

681 "DP Audit Uncovers $289,000 Fraud." **EDPACS,** 6, no. 6 (Dec. 1978), p. 14.

682 "DP Crime Bill Gets Liberal Support." **Computerworld,** 17, no. 37 (12 Sept. 1983), p. 15.

683 "DPer Charged with Forgery." **Computerworld,** 16, no. 2 (11 Jan. 1982), p. 29.

684 "Dann v. Johnston: Program Patentability Postponed." **Detroit College of Law Review**, 1976, no. 3 (1976), pp. 663–74.

685 "Data Processing Needs a Bigger Security Blanket." **Modern Office Procedures**, 25 (July 1980), p. 68.

686 David, R.M. "Privacy and Security in Data Systems." **Computers and People**, 23 (March 1974), pp. 20–27.

687 Davidson, Duncan M. "Constructing OEM Nondisclosure Agreements." **Jurimetrics Journal**, 24, no. 2 (Winter 1984), pp. 127–53.

688 _____. "Negotiating Major System Procurements." **Computer/Law Journal**, 3 (Spring 1982), pp. 385–426.

689 _____. "Project Controls in Computer Contracting." **Computer/Law Journal**, 4, no. 1 (Summer 1983), pp. 133–58.

690 _____. "Protecting Computer Software: A Comprehensive Analysis." **Arizona State Law Journal**, 1983, no. 4 (1983), pp. 611–784.

691 _____. "Protecting Computer Software: A Comprehensive Analysis." **Jurimetrics Journal**, 23, no. 4 (Summer 1983), pp. 337–425.

692 Davidson, Mark. "Computer Privacy." **Science Digest**, 82, no. 3 (Sept. 1977), pp. 42–44.

693 Davis, Harold L. "Computer Programs and Subject Matter Patentability." **Rutgers Journal of Computers and the Law**, 6, no. 1 (1977), pp. 1–25.

694 Davis, Ruth M. "Implications of Privacy Legislation on the Use of Computer Technology in Business." **Jurimetrics Journal**, 17, no. 1 (Fall 1976), pp. 95–110.

695 _____. "Privacy and Security in Data Systems." **Computers and People**, 23, no. 3 (Mar. 1974), pp. 20–27.

696 _____. "A Technologist's View of Privacy and Security in Automated Information Systems." **Rutgers Journal**

of Computers and the Law, 4, no. 2 (1975), pp. 264-82.

697 "Dectape Patent Decision Overturned." **Computerworld,** 15, no. 28 (13 July 1981), p. 75.

698 "Defender II Safeguards Data Bases." **Computerworld,** 17, no. 41 (10 Oct. 1983), p. 72.

699 De Gouw, Chris. "Data Processing Crimes." **EDPACS,** 5, no. 7 (Jan. 1978), pp. 1-8.

700 Demitriades, P.B. "Administrative Secrecy and Data Privacy Legislation." **Journal of Systems Management,** 27 (Oct. 1976), pp. 24-29.

701 Dent, Ike. "Legislation Proposed Against Computer Fraud." **The Credit World,** 66 (Feb. 1978), p. 11.

702 DeRensis, Paul R. "The Civil Liabilities of Data Base Operators." **The Practical Lawyer,** 24, no. 5 (July 1978), pp. 25-38.

703 "Details on Fed Data Theft." **The New York Times,** 132 (12 Jan. 1983), pp. D1, D8.

704 "The Development of Canadian Law on Transborder Data Flow." **Georgia Journal of International and Comparative Law,** 13 (Summer 1983), pp. 825-55.

705 "Device for Dial-Up Data Bases Arrests Unauthorized Access." **Computerworld,** 16, no. 45 (8 Nov. 1982), p. 79.

706 DeWeese, J. Taylor. "Giving the Computer a Conscience." **Harper's,** 247, no. 1482 (Nov. 1973), pp. 14, 16-17.

707 _____. "Reforming Our 'Record Prisons': A Proposal for the Federal Regulation of Crime Data Banks." **Rutgers-Camden Law Journal,** 6, no. 1 (Summer 1974), pp. 26-83.

708 _____. "The Trojan Horse Caper—And Assorted Other Computer Crimes." **Saturday Review,** 3, no. 4 (15 Nov. 1975), pp. 10, 58-60.

709 "Dialing for Data—Illegally." **Newsweek,** 101, no. 3 (17 Jan. 1983), p. 54.

710 "Dial-Up Lines Get Security." **Computerworld,** 17, no. 16 (18 Apr. 1983), p. 65.

711 "Diamond v. Diehr: A Step Towards Computer Program Patentability?" **Detroit College of Law Review,** 1982, no. 1 (Spring 1982), pp. 127-46.

712 "Diamond v. Diehr, II: The Patentability of Inventions Utilizing a Mathematical Algorithm or Computer Program--Related Inventions." **South Texas Law Journal,** 23, no. 1 (Winter 1982), pp. 224-33.

713 "Diamond v. Diehr: The Patentability of Processes and Incorporated Algorithms." **Ohio Northern University Law Review,** 8, no. 1 (1981), pp. 535-42.

714 "Diamond v. Diehr: The Supreme Court Confronts the Future." **The Journal of Law and Commerce,** 3 (1983), pp. 143-65.

715 Dietz, Lawrence D. "Computer Security: Not Just for Mainframes." **Mini-Micro Systems,** 15, no. 6 (June 1982), p. 251.

716 "The Dissemination of Arrest Records and the Iowa Tracis Bill." **Iowa Law Review,** 59, no. 5 (June 1974), pp. 1162-93.

717 Dixon, David J. "Legal Problems of Data Base Technology." **Washington University Law Quarterly,** 1977, no. 3 (Summer 1977), pp. 537-40.

718 Donlan, Thomas G. "Social Security Scam: Only a Stroke of Luck Uncovered Mrs. Blair." **Barrons** (18 Aug. 1980), pp. 9+.

719 Donnici, Peter J. "Consumers' Right to Privacy in Electronic Fund Transfers: Some Concluding Observations." **University of San Francisco Law Review,** 13, no. 2 (Winter 1979), pp. 549-53.

720 Dorr, Robert C., and William P. Eigles. "Resolving Claims to Ownership of Software and Computer-Stored Data— The Importance of Temporary Restraining Orders and Preliminary Injunctions." **Computer/Law Journal,** 5, no. 1 (Summer 1984), pp. 1-24.

721 "The Dossier Problem." **Scientific American,** 239, no. 1 (July 1978), p. 72.

722 Dotto, Lydia. "The Age of the Electronic Rip-Off." **Canadian Business,** 52, no. 6 (June 1979), pp. 54, 56, 59-64.

723 _____. "The New Computer Criminals." **Atlas World Press Review,** 26, no. 8 (Aug. 1979), pp. 25-26.

724 Douglas, James. "Some Ideas on the Computer and the Law." **Texas Southern University Law Review,** 2 (1972-73), pp. 20-37.

725 Draper, Hayward L. "Privacy and Police Intelligence Data Banks: A Proposal to Create a State Organized Crime Intelligence System and to Regulate the Use of Criminal Intelligence Information." **Harvard Journal on Legislation,** 14, no. 1 (Dec. 1976), pp. 1-110.

726 "Drugs, Databanks, and Dignity: Computerized Selection of Travelers for Intrusive Border Searches." **Boston University Law Review,** 56, no. 5 (Nov. 1976), pp. 940-69.

727 Ducker, Bruce. "Liability for Computer Software." **The Business Lawyer,** 26, no. 4 (Apr. 1971), pp. 1081-94.

728 Duggan, Michael A. "Patents on Programs? The Supreme Court Says No." **Jurimetrics Journal,** 13, no. 3 (Spring 1973), pp. 135-38.

729 Duncan, Gaylen A. "Business and Economic Implications of Programme Patent Protection in Canada." **Computer/ Law Journal,** 1, no. 1 (Spring 1978), pp. 105-88.

730 Dunner, Donald R., James B. Gambrell, Stuart A. White, and Irving Kayton. "Nonstatutory Subject Matter." **Jurimetrics Journal,** 14, no. 2 (Winter 1973), pp. 113-23.

731 Dunning, Matthew. "Some Aspects of Theft of Computer Software." **Auckland University Law Review,** 4, no. 3 (1982), pp. 273-94.

732 Durham, W. Cole, Jr. "The Modification of Law Under the Influence of Computer Technology." **The American Journal of Comparative Law,** 30, (1982), pp. 601-19.

733 "EFT Act Favors Consumers, But Has Some Curves." **Computer Law and Tax Report**, 5, no. 8 (Mar. 1979), pp. 3-5.

734 "EFT and Privacy." **Federal Reserve Bulletin**, 64, no. 4 (Apr. 1978), pp. 279-84.

735 "EFT Fraud: Who Will Pay?" **The Banker**, 132, no. 673 (Mar. 1982), pp. 11-12.

736 "EFT Systems and Privacy." **The Journal of Accountancy**, 146, no. 4 (Oct. 1978), p. 104.

737 "Easing Plaintiffs' Burden of Proving Negligence for Computer Malfunction." **Iowa Law Review**, 69, no. 1 (Oct. 1983), pp. 241-62.

738 "Editorial Comment: Inside Operators." **National Underwriters Property Edition**, 78, no. 30 (26 July 1974), p. 16.

739 "The Effect of the Statute of Limitations on a Computer Vendor's Liability in a Failed Computer Installation: Triangle Underwriters, Inc. v. Honeywell, Inc." **Saint Louis University Law Journal**, 26, no. 1 (1981), pp. 181-202.

740 Ege, Stephen M. "Electronic Funds Transfer: A Survey of Problems and Prospects in 1975." **Maryland Law Review**, 35, no. 1 (1975), pp. 3-56.

741 Eger, John. "The Role of the Federal Reserve in Electronic Funds Transfer—An Executive Perspective." **Catholic University Law Review**, 25, no. 4 (Summer 1976), pp. 739-48.

742 _____. "Transborder Data Flow." **Datamation**, 24, no. 12 (15 Nov. 1978), pp. 50, 52, 54.

743 Eger, John M. "Emerging Restrictions on Transnational Data Flows: Privacy Protection or Non-Tariff Trade Barriers?" **Law and Policy in International Business**, 10, no. 4 (1978), pp. 1055-1103.

744 _____. "The Global Phenomenon of Teleinformatics: An Introduction." **Cornell International Law Journal**, 14, no. 2 (Summer 1981), pp. 203-36.

745 "Electronic Data Processing in Private Hospitals: Patient Privacy, Confidentiality and Control." **Suffolk University Law Review,** 13, no. 5 (Fall 1979), pp. 1386-1429.

746 "Electronic Fund Transfer in Iowa: Implications for the Regulation of Competition Among Federal and State Financial Institutions." **Iowa Law Review,** 61, no. 5 (June 1976), pp. 1355-1402.

747 "Electronic Fund Transfers, Branch Banks, and Potential Abuse of Privacy." **Fordham Urban Law Journal,** 6 (Spring 1977-78), pp. 571-97.

748 "Electronic Fund Transfers: Regulation E and the Right to Privacy." **Gonzaga Law Review,** 16, no. 2 (1981), pp. 313-55.

749 "Electronic Funds Transfer." **The Business Lawyer,** 32, no. 1 (Nov. 1976), pp. 201-46.

750 "Electronic Funds Transfer Systems: A Need for New Law." **New England Law Review,** 12, no. 1 (Summer 1976), pp. 111-34.

751 Ellison, Ray. "The Changing Face of the 'Fraudsman'." **The CPA Journal,** 46, no. 1 (Jan. 1976), pp. 5-6.

752 Elmer-Dewitt, Philip. "Cracking Down—Hackers Face Tough New Laws." **Time,** 123 (14 May 1984), p. 83.

753 _____. "The 414 Gang Strikes Again." **Time,** 122 (29 Aug. 1983), p. 75.

754 "Embezzling Case at Wells Fargo: Keys Are Computer and Volume." **The New York Times,** 130 (23 Feb. 1981), pp. A1, B5.

755 "Employee Faces Theft Charges for CAD System." **Computerworld,** 16, no. 30 (26 July 1982), p. 12.

756 "Encryption: Can Spies and Thieves Break It?" **Technology Review,** 85, no. 8 (Nov.-Dec. 1982), pp. 72-74.

757 Ervin, Sam J. "The Final Answer: The People in Control." **Trial,** 7, no. 2 (Mar.-Apr. 1971), pp. 14-17, 28.

758 Evans, A.C. "Data Protection in Europe." **Journal of World Trade Law,** 15, (1981), pp. 150-58.

759 _____. "European Data Protection Law." **The American Journal of Comparative Law,** 29, no. 4 (Fall 1981), pp. 571-82.

760 Evans, Andrew. "Computers and Privacy: The New Council of Europe Convention." **New Law Journal,** 130, no. 5976 (13 Nov. 1980), pp. 1067-68.

761 Ewald, Thomas R. "Discovery and the Computer." **Litigation,** 1, no. 2 (Spring 1975), pp. 27-31.

762 "Examples of Computer Crime Listed in Guide." **The National Underwriter,** 84, no. 21 (24 May 1980), p. 7.

763 "Expert Identifies Crime Scenarios." **Computerworld,** 16, no. 28 (12 July 1982), p. 11.

764 "Experts Say Computerization Raises Risk of Embezzlement." **The Wall Street Journal,** 197, no. 36 (23 Feb. 1981), p. 25.

765 "Exxon Chips Worth $2 Million Stolen." **Computerworld,** 16, no. 9 (1 Mar. 1982), p. 2.

766 "FBI Levels Sights on Computer Crimes." **Administrative Management,** 40, no. 3 (Mar. 1979), p. 22.

767 "FDIC and Comptroller's Office Issue Guidelines on How Banks Should Protect Against EFT Fraud." **Banking,** 69, no. 1 (Jan. 1977), pp. 37+.

768 Faflick, Philip, Russell Leavitt, and Marlin Levin. "Opening the 'Trapdoor Knapsack'." **Time,** 120, no. 17 (25 Oct. 1982), p. 88.

769 Farley, Andrew N. "Computers--Data--Privacy: A Mobius Effect." **Pennsylvania Bar Association Quarterly,** 47, no. 4 (Oct. 1976), pp. 545-53.

770 "Federal Home Loan Bank Board Adopts EFT Rules." **Computer Law and Tax Report,** 4, no. 12 (July 1978), p. 6.

771 "Federal Record Poor for Privacy Protection." **Computer-world,** 17/18, nos. 52/1 (26 Dec. 1983/2 Jan. 1984), p. 87.

772 "Federal Unfair Competition Act Proposed." **Computer Law and Tax Report,** 4, no. 1 (Aug. 1977), p. 3.

773 "Feds Expected to Squelch 'Gray Market'." **Computerworld,** 16/17, nos. 52/1, (27 Dec. 1982/3 Jan. 1983), p. 74.

774 "Fedwire Theft Fails." **EDPACS,** 6, no. 4 (Oct. 1978), p. 11.

775 Feistel, Horst. "Cryptography and Computer Privacy." **Scientific American,** 228, no. 5 (May 1973), pp. 15-23.

776 Felsman, Robert A., et al. "Computer Program Protection." **Texas Bar Journal,** 34, no. 1 (22 Jan. 1971), pp. 33-56, 58-61.

777 Fetherling, Doug. "A New Breed of Thief." **Canadian Business,** 53, supp.: **Focus,** 1, no. 7 (Sept. 1980), pp. 9-10, 14.

778 "Final Report of the National Commission on New Technological Uses of Copyrighted Works (July 31, 1978): Sections on Software Copyrights." **Computer/Law Journal,** 3 (Fall 1981), pp. 53-104.

779 "Financial Privacy in an Electronic Fund Transfer Environment: An Analysis of the Right to Financial Privacy Act of 1978 and California Financial Privacy Law." **University of San Francisco Law Review,** 13, no. 2 (Winter 1979), pp. 485-503.

780 "Firm Bolsters DP Security with Risk Analysis." **Computerworld,** 16, no. 26 (28 June 1982), p. SR 40.

781 "Firms See DP Security as Expense, Not Benefit, Says Law Specialist." **Computerworld,** 17, no. 29 (18 July 1983), p. 17.

782 "Firmware May Be Patentable." **Computer Law and Tax Report,** 6, no. 4 (Nov. 1979), p. 4.

783 Flewellen, Linda Nell. "An Anomaly in the Patent System: The Uncertain Status of Computer Software." **Rutgers Journal of Computers, Technology and Law,** 8, no. 2 (1981), pp. 273-303.

784 "Florida Computer Crime Bill Creates Problems." **Computer Law and Tax Report,** 5, no. 5 (Dec. 1978), pp. 5-6.

785 "For Fun or Foul, Computer Hackers Can Crack Any Code." **The Wall Street Journal,** 201, no. 72 (13 Apr. 1983), p. 1.

786 "Former Employee Charged with Tapping Fed's Data Bank." **Computerworld,** 17, no. 2 (10 Jan. 1983), p. 11.

787 Forst, Martin, and David Weckler. "Research Access into Automated Criminal Justice Information Systems and the Right to Privacy." **University of San Fernando Valley Law Review,** 5, no. 2 (Fall 1977), pp. 321-65.

788 "Four Nations to Study DP, Privacy, Security." **Computer Decisions,** 10, no. 2 (Feb. 1978), p. 6.

789 Fowler, Elizabeth M. "Detecting Computer Criminals." **The New York Times,** 129 (18 June 1980), p. D15.

790 "France Is Ready to Clamp Down on Computer Abuse of Privacy." **Datamation,** 23 (April 1977), pp. 162-164.

791 Frank, Robert J. "The Patentability of Software Inventions." **IEEE Spectrum,** 15, no. 4 (Apr. 1978), pp. 42-46.

792 Frank, Werner L. "Beware of Advice from Experts About Software." **Computerworld,** 15, no. 34 (24 Aug. 1981), pp. 31, 34.

793 Franklin, J. Thomas. "Proprietary Protection of Computer Data Bases." **Computer Law Service,** 3, §4-4, art. 3 (1973), pp. 1-9.

794 "Frankly, Incredible: Unconscionability in Computer Contracts." **Computer/Law Journal,** 4, no. 4 (Spring 1984), pp. 695-736.

795 Frantz, Al. "The Big Computer 'Con'." **The Journal of Insurance,** 40, no. 2 (Mar.-Apr. 1979), pp. 34-39.

796 "Fraud: Conning by Computer." **Newsweek,** 89, no. 17 (23 Apr. 1973), pp. 90, 93.

797 Freed, Roy N. "Computer Records and the Law—Retrospect and Prospect." **Jurimetrics Journal**, 15, no. 3 (Spring 1975), pp. 207-9.

798 _____. "Legal Aspects of Computers and Confidentiality." **Jurimetrics Journal**, 18, no. 4 (Summer 1978), pp. 328-334.

799 _____. "Products Liability in the Computer Age." **Forum**, 12, no. 2 (Winter 1977), pp. 461-78.

800 _____. "Products Liability in the Computer Age." **Jurimetrics Journal**, 17, no. 4 (Summer 1977), pp. 270-85.

801 _____. "Protection of Proprietary Programs in Light of Benson and Tabbot." **Jurimetrics Journal**, 13, no. 3 (Spring 1973), pp. 139-41.

802 _____. "Security Interests in the Computer Age: Practical Advice for the Secured Lender." **The Banking Law Journal**, 101, no. 5 (July-Aug. 1984), pp. 404-29.

803 _____. "Software Protection: Introductory Observations on the Study Sponsored by the National Commission on New Technological Uses of Copyrighted Works." **Jurimetrics Journal**, 18, no. 4 (Summer 1978), pp. 352-53.

804 Freedman, Warren. "The Right of Privacy in the Age of Computer Data and Processing." **Texas Tech Law Review**, 13, no. 4 (1982), pp. 1361-1400.

805 "French President Goes on TV to Announce Development of Antiterrorist Data Base." **Computerworld**, 16, no. 34 (23 Aug. 1982), p. 2.

806 Frenkel, Karen A. "Computers in Court." **Technology Review**, 85, no. 3 (Apr. 1982), pp. 28-29.

807 Friedman, Robert. "The Dalton Gang's Computer Caper." **New York**, 13, no. 48 (8 Dec. 1980), pp. 65-75.

808 Fromholz, Haley J. "Discovery, Evidence, Confidentiality, and Security Problems Associated with the Use of Computer-Based Litigation Support Systems." **Washington University Law Quarterly**, 1977, no. 3 (Summer 1977), pp. 445-60.

809 Furner, Joanne F., and J. Wm. Thomason. "Physician—
Patient Confidences: Legal Effects of Computerization
of Records." **The Alabama Lawyer,** 31, no. 2 (Apr. 1970),
pp. 193-202.

810 Gaines, R. Stockton, and Norman Z. Shapiro. "Some Security Principles and Their Application to Computer Security." **ACM Operating System Review,** 12, no. 3 (July
1978), pp. 19-28.

811 Galbi, Elmer. "Proposal for New Legislation to Protect
Computer Programming." **Bulletin of the Copyright Society of the U.S.A.,** 17, no. 4 (Apr. 1970), pp. 280-96.

812 Galbi, Elmer W. "The Aftermath of the Benson and Tabbot
Decision." **Computer Law Service,** 3, §4-2, art. 2 (1979),
pp. 1-7.

813 _____. "Copyright Law and the Protection of Computer
Programming." **Computer Law Service,** 3, §4-3, art. 1
(1979), pp. 1-18.

814 _____. "The Prospect of Future Legislation and Court
Action Concerning the Protection of Programming."
Jurimetrics Journal, 13, no. 4 (Summer 1973), pp. 234-39.

815 Gallant, John. "Pa. Law to Provide Stiff Penalities for
Hackers." **Computerworld,** 18, no. 5 (30 Jan. 1984), p. 13.

816 _____. "Reformers Argue '68 Law Leaves Data Vulnerable." **Computerworld,** 18, no. 5 (30 Jan. 1984), p. 6.

817 Galler, Elaine. B. "Contracting Problems in the Computer
Industry: Should Computer Specialists Be Subjected to
Malpractice Liability." **Insurance Counsel Journal,** 50,
no. 4 (Oct. 1983), pp. 574-98.

818 Gammer, Michele. "White Collar Crime: A Survey of Law.
Computer Crime." **American Criminal Law Review,** 18,
no. 2 (Fall 1980), pp. 370-86.

819 "Garbage In, Gospel Out: Establishing Probable Cause
Through Computerized Criminal Information Transmit-
tals." **The Hastings Law Journal,** 28, no. 2 (Nov. 1976),
pp. 509-31.

820 Garland, John L. "Computers and the Law in the 1980's." **Law and Computer Technology,** 8, no. 3 (May-June 1975), pp. 62-77.

821 Garretson, Monty. "Think Like a Crook." **Best's Review Life/Health Insurance Edition,** 83, no. 10 (Feb. 1983), pp. 74+.

822 Gates, Patrick O. "How Can Accountants and Auditors Prevent Computer Fraud?" **The Government Accountants Journal,** 28, no. 2 (Summer 1978), pp. 10-15.

823 Gavrilov, E.P. "New Technology and Copyright Law." **Soviet Law and Government,** 22, no. 2 (Fall 1983), pp. 33-44.

824 Gellmann, H.S. "Using the Computer to Steal." **Journal of Systems Management,** 25, no. 10 (Oct. 1974), pp. 28-32.

825 Gellmann, Harvey S. "Using the Computer to Steal." **Computers and Automation,** 20, no. 4 (Apr. 1971), pp. 16-19.

826 Gemignani, Michael. "Computer Crime: The Law in '80." **Indiana Law Review,** 13, no. 3 (1980), pp. 681-723.

827 _____. "Should Algorithms Be Patentable?" **Jurimetrics Journal,** 22, no. 3 (Spring 1982), pp. 326-36.

828 Gemignani, Michael C. "Legal Protection for Computer Software: The View from '79." **Rutgers Journal of Computers, Technology and the Law,** 7, no. 2 (1980), pp. 269-312.

829 _____. "Product Liability and Software." **Rutgers Journal of Computers, Technology and the Law,** 8, no. 2 (1981), pp. 173-204.

830 _____. "Who's to Blame When the Program Fails? Theories in Programmer Liability--Part 1." **Computerworld,** 15, no. 45 (9 Nov. 1981), pp. ID 33-36.

831 _____. "Who's to Blame When the Program Fails? Theories in Programmer Liability--Part 2." **Computerworld,** 15, no. 46 (16 Nov. 1981), pp. ID 15-16, 18-20.

832 _____. "Who's to Blame When the Program Fails? Theories in Programmer Liability--Part 3." **Computerworld,** 15, no. 47 (23 Nov. 1981), pp. ID 11-14.

833 _____. "Who's to Blame When the Program Fails? Theories in Programmer Liability—Part 4." **Computerworld,** 15, no. 48 (30 Nov. 1981), pp. ID 11, 14-16.

834 "Get the Bugs Out of Your System Before a Jury Gets Involved." **Computer Law and Tax Report,** 4, no. 9 (Apr. 1978), p. 6.

835 "Getting Tough on Software Theft." **Business Week,** no. 2741 (31 May 1982), pp. 28-29.

836 Gilbert, Harvey, and Jonathan Joseph. "Software Piracy." **Computerworld,** 16, no. 19 (10 May 1982), pp. ID 1-5, 8-9.

837 Gilburne, Miles R., and Ronald L. Johnston. "Trade Secret Protection for Software Generally and in the Mass Market." **Computer/Law Journal,** 3 (Spring 1982), pp. 211-72.

838 Gillin, Paul. "Banks 'Leaving Doors Wide Open' to Disastrous Computer Crimes, DP Security Expert Warns." **Computerworld,** 17, no. 24 (13 June 1983), pp. 20-21.

839 _____. "Court Upholds Apple's ROM Copyright Suit." **Computerworld,** 17, no. 37 (12 Sept. 1983), p. 5.

840 _____. "DP Crime-for-Profit Scheme Rocks Texas Court." **Computerworld,** 16, no. 45 (8 Nov. 1982), p. 9.

841 _____. "Danger of Electronic Theft Seen Escalating." **Computerworld,** 17, no. 47 (21 Nov. 1983), p. 25.

842 _____. "Judge Awards $250,000 to Software Developers." **Computerworld,** 16, no. 39 (27 Sept. 1982), p. 106.

843 _____. "Supreme Court Decision Seen as Win for Software Houses." **Computerworld,** 17, no. 2, (10 Jan. 1983), pp. 65,68.

844 Golden, Frederic, and Philip Faflick. "Superzapping in Computer Land." **Time,** 117, no. 2 (12 Jan. 1981), p. 76.

845 Goldstein, R.C. "Costs of Privacy." **Datamation,** 21 (Oct. 1975), pp. 65-69.

846 Goldstein, Robert C., and Richard L. Nolan. "Personal Privacy Versus the Corporate Computer." **Harvard Business Review,** 53, no. 2 (Mar.-Apr. 1975), pp. 62-70.

847 Golsong, Heribert. "Towards a European Convention on
Data Protection." **Computer Networks,** 3, no. 3 (June
1979), pp. 205-14.

848 Gomes, L. "Secrets of the Software Pirates." **Esquire,** 97
(Jan. 1982), pp. 58-65.

849 Gordon, Hedy. "The Interface of Living Systems and Computers: The Legal Issues of Privacy." **Computer/Law
Journal,** 2, no. 4 (Fall 1980), pp. 877-90.

850 Gorenstein, Charles. "The Dual Standard of Patentability:
A New Look at the Computer Issue." **Journal of the Patent Office Society,** 62, no. 2 (Feb. 1980), pp. 96-107.

851 Gorman, James. "Computer Capers." **Datamation,** 23, no.
3 (Mar. 1977), pp. 105-6.

852 Gottheimer, Debra. "Those Hidden Opportunities for Computer Crime." **Administrative Management,** 39, no. 1
(Jan. 1978), pp. 65+.

853 "Gottschalk v. Benson: A Bright Light with a Dim Future."
Baylor Law Review, 28, no. 1 (Winter 1976), pp. 187-95.

854 "Government Is Lax on Computer Security." **Office,** 84
(July 1976), pp. 66+.

855 Grayson, B. "Computer Crimebusters." **Black Enterprise,**
12 (May 1982), pp. 59-60.

856 Green, Jeffrey D. "How to Fend Off Computer Culprits."
("Business Forum"). **The New York Times,** 133 (29 Jan.
1984), sec. 3, p. 3, col. 1.

857 Greenberg, David H. "Your Legal Rights to the Software
You Create and Buy." **Administrative Management,** 34,
no. 9 (Sept. 1973), p. 35.

858 Greene, Richard. "Beep Beep—Call a Lawyer." **Forbes,** 131,
no. 8 (11 Apr. 1983), p. 51.

859 Greenfield, John W. "Computers: How to Protect Your
Rights When You Buy One." **Architectural Record,** 171,
no. 4 (Apr. 1983), pp. 43, 45.

860 Greer, Philip, and Myron Kandel. "Corporations Adding Security Against Data Thefts." **New York Law Journal,** 183, no. 27 (7 Feb. 1980), p. 4.

861 Greguras, Fred. "Electronic Funds Transfers and the Financial Institution/Consumer Relationship." **Uniform Commerical Code Law Journal,** 10, no. 3 (Winter 1978), pp. 172-221.

862 Greguras, Fred M. "The Allocation of Risk in Electronic Fund Transfer Systems for Losses Caused by Unauthorized Transactions." **University of San Francisco Law Review,** 13, no. 2 (Winter 1979), pp. 405-29.

863 _____, and Ann L. Wright. "How the New EFT Act Affects the Financial Institution/Consumer Relationship." **Uniform Commercial Code Law Journal,** 11, no. 3 (Winter 1979), pp. 207-71.

864 _____, and David J. Sykes. "Authentication in EFT: The Legal Standard and the Operational Reality." **Computer/ Law Journal,** 2, no. 1 (Winter 1980), pp. 67-86.

865 Grenier, Edward J., Jr. "Computers and Privacy: A Proposal for Self-Regulation." **Duke Law Journal,** 1970, no. 3 (June 1970), pp. 495-513.

866 Grimes, John A. "Equity Funding: Fraud by Computer." **The American Federationist,** 80, no. 12 (Dec. 1973), pp. 7-10.

867 Grogan, Allen R. "Some Face Copyright Forfeiture by Dec. 31." **Computerworld,** 16, no. 45 (8 Nov. 1982), pp. 115, 124.

868 Groshan, Robert M. "Transnational Data Flows: Is the Idea of an International Legal Regime Relevant in Establishing Multilateral Controls and Legal Norms? Part One." **Law/Technology,** 14, no. 4 (4th Quarter 1981), pp. 1-30.

869 _____. "Transnational Data Flows: Is the Idea of an International Legal Regime Relevant in Establishing Multilateral Controls and Legal Norms? Part Two." **Law/ Technology,** 15, no. 1 (1st Quarter 1982), pp. 1-37.

870 Grosswirth, Marvin. "How Credit Card Crooks Pick Your Pocket." **Science Digest,** 77, no. 6 (June 1975), pp. 58-65.

871 "Growing Problems." **USA Today,** 111, no. 2449 (Oct. 1982), p. 14.

872 "The Growing Threat to Computer Security." **Business Week,** no. 2494 (1 Aug. 1977), pp. 44-45.

873 "Guarding Against Computer Fraud." **Banking,** 68 (Apr. 1976), pp. 36+.

874 Guthrie, David W. "Computer Law: A California Perspective." **Lincoln Law Review,** 12, no. 2 (1981), pp. 103-112.

875 "HEW Establishes Antifraud Record System." **Computer Law and Tax Report,** 5, no. 8 (Mar. 1979), p. 7.

876 "Habeas Data: The Right of Privacy Versus Computer Surveillance." **University of San Francisco Law Review,** 5, no. 2 (Apr. 1971), pp. 358-77.

877 Hafner, Katherine. "Class Action Suit Blames False Arrests on L.A.'s System." **Computerworld,** 17, no. 15 (11 Apr. 1983), pp. 20-21.

878 _____. "Felony Charges Filed Against Alleged Hacker." **Computerworld,** 17, no. 46 (14 Nov. 1983), p. 15.

879 Haines, Brian W. "No Copyright in Computer Software?" **Solicitors' Journal,** 128, no. 8 (24 Feb. 1984), pp. 126-127.

880 Halls, Craig C. "Raiding the Databanks: A Developing Problem for Technologists and Lawyers." **Journal of Contemporary Law,** 5, no. 2 (Spring 1979), pp. 245-66.

881 Halper, Stanley. "How to Thwart Computer Criminals." **Nations Business,** 71, no. 8 (Aug. 1983), pp. 61-62.

882 _____. "Lax Controls Over Computers a Threat to Law Firms." **New York Law Journal,** 185, no. 66 (7 Apr. 1981), p. 3, col. 1.

883 Hamburg, C. Bruce. "Inventions Relating to Computers or Use Thereof Again Being Considered by U.S. Supreme Court." **Patent and Trademark Review,** 78, no. 12 (Dec. 1980), pp. 518-21.

884 _____. "U.S. Supreme Court Affirms CCPA in Two

Cases According Patent Protection to Inventions Relating to Computers." **Patent and Trademark Review,**
79, no. 5 (May 1981), pp. 211-14.

885 Hammer, Carl. "Computer Program Protection." **Idea,** 14
(1970), pp. 10-13.

886 Hammer, Robert J. "Protecting the Agency from Computer Theft and Fraud." **Best's Review—Property/Casualty
Insurance Edition,** 83, no. 3 (July 1982), pp. 70, 72-73.

887 Hammond, James H., Jr. "Guarding the Gate: Data Processing Security." **Mortgage Banking,** 43, no. 7 (Apr. 1983),
pp. 27-28+.

888 Harris, Charles Edison. "Complex Contract Issues in the
Acquisition of Hardware and Software." **Computer/Law
Journal,** 4, no. 1 (Summer 1983), pp. 77-100.

889 Harris, John R. "Apple Computer, Inc. v. Franklin Computer Corp.—Does a ROM a Computer Program Make?"
Jurimetrics Journal, 24, no. 3 (Spring 1984), pp. 248-53.

890 Hassett, Robert W. "Some Procedures for Copyright Registration." **Computerworld,** 17, no. 42 (17 Oct. 1983), pp.
50-52.

891 Heller, C.E. "EFT and the Prospects for Individual Privacy."
Datamation, 21 (Sept. 1975), pp. 174+.

892 Henderson, Bruce, and Jeffrey Young. "The Heist." **Esquire,**
95, no. 5 (May 1981), pp. 36-47.

893 Henderson, Robert. "A False Fear." **Trial,** 7, no. 2 (Mar.-
Apr. 1971), pp. 24-25.

894 Henkel, Tom. "B80 User Wins Half a Million from Burroughs." **Computerworld,** 15, no. 25 (22 June 1981), pp. 1, 7.

895 _____. "Ex-Bus Scheduler Acquitted of Extortion after
Asking Payment for Programs." **Computerworld,** 17, no.
24 (13 June 1983), p. 2.

896 _____. "High-Level IBMers Accused of Trying to Sell
Micro Secrets." **Computerworld,** 16, no. 38 (20 Sept. 1982),
pp. 1, 4.

897 _____. "Hired Hacker Not New Phenomenon to Geisco." Computerworld, 17, no. 40 (3 Oct. 1983), p. 13.

898 _____. "Insurer Decides to Ensure DP Operation." Computerworld, 15, no. 37 (7 Sept. 1981), pp. 59-60.

899 _____. "Radio Waves from Your System Giving Away Your Secrets?" Computerworld, 17, no. 19 (9 May 1983), pp. 1, 10.

900 _____. "St. Louis Institutes Computer Crime Divison." Computerworld, 17, no. 16 (18 Apr. 1983), p. 33.

901 _____. "Security Experts Raise Red Flag About End Users' Floppy Disks." Computerworld, 17, no. 29 (18 July 1983), pp. 1, 10.

902 _____. "User Suits Give Rise to 'Malpractice' Insurance." Computerworld, 17, no. 39 (26 Sept. 1983), p. 24.

903 Henriques, Vico E. "Guilty, Not Guilty, or Not so Guilty?" Technology Review, 85, no. 3 (Apr. 1982), pp. 24-25.

904 Herman, Edward S. "Equity Funding, Inside Information, and the Regulators." U.C.L.A. Law Review, 21, no. 1 (Oct. 1973), pp. 1-28.

905 "The High-Tech Threat to Your Privacy." Changing Times, 37, no. 4 (Apr. 1983), pp. 60, 62-63.

906 Hirsch, Phil. "Amendments Proposed for Rewrite of 1934 Act." Computerworld, 15, no. 29 (20 July 1981), pp. 11-12.

907 _____. "Cbema Claims S.898, Senate Rewrite Bill, Fails to Protect Present Private-Line Users." Computerworld, 15, no. 28 (13 July 1981), p. 72.

908 _____. "Committee Head Proposes H.R. 5158 Changes." Computerworld, 16, no. 18 (3 May 1982), p. 9.

909 _____. "Communications Bill Goes to House Floor." Computerworld, 15, no. 50 (14 Dec. 1981), p. 5.

910 _____. "H.R. 5158 Abandoned." Computerworld, 16, no. 30 (26 July 1982), p. 1.

911 _____. "IBM's Cary Warns Against Industry Cynicism."
      Computerworld, 16, no. 46 (15 Nov. 1982), p. 15.

912 _____. "Olson Blasts H.R. 5158 as Anti-Competitive."
      Computerworld, 16, no. 24 (14 June 1982), p. 17.

913 "Hitachi Defense Mum on IBM Payment Report." **Comput-
      erworld,** 17, no. 47 (21 Nov. 1983), p. 104.

914 "Hitachi, NAS to Turn Over Allegedly Stolen Material."
      Computerworld, 16, no. 46 (15 Nov. 1982), p. 4.

915 Hoard, Bruce. "Bell Watchers Hoist Warning Flag Over
      Patents." **Computerworld,** 16, no. 35 (30 Aug. 1982), p. 4.

916 _____. "Computer Mix-Up Puts Woman in Limbo." **Com-
      puterworld,** 16, no. 19 (10 May 1982), p. 24.

917 _____. "Court Upholds Ruling on Software Tangibility."
      Computerworld, 16, no. 30 (26 July 1982), p. 15.

918 _____. "IEEE 802 Hits Patent Snag; IBM Solved Same
      Problem by Shelling Out $5 Million." **Computerworld,** 16,
      no. 36 (6 Sept. 1982), p. 5.

919 Hoffman, Paul S. "Computer Contracts—A Lawyer's Prim-
      er." **New York State Bar Journal,** 51, no. 6 (Oct. 1979),
      pp. 470-73.

920 Holder, John E. "Computer Program Protection. IV. Trade
      Secrets." **Texas Bar Journal,** 34, no. 1 (Jan. 1971), pp. 53-
      59.

921 Hollander, Patricia A. "An Introduction to Legal and Ethi-
      cal Issues Relating to Computers in Higher Education."
      The Journal of College and University Law, 11, no. 2
      (Fall 1984), pp. 215-32.

922 Holliday, Linda L. "Protecting Computer Software."
      Louisiana Bar Journal, 32, no. 2 (Aug. 1984), pp. 90-93,
      96-98.

923 Hollis, G. "Basics of Computer Security." **Accountancy,** 88
      (Jan. 1977), pp. 108+.

924 Holmes. "Software Security." **Journal of Systems Management,** 24 (Sept. 1973), p. 18.

925 Hook, Elizabeth. "New Lloyd's Computer Crime Policy Takes Risk Management Approach." **Risk Management,** 29, no. 2 (Feb. 1982), pp. 57-58.

926 Hope, Henry W. "Computer Program Protection. III. Copyright Protection." **Texas Bar Journal,** 34, no. 1 (Jan. 1971), pp. 35-53.

927 "House, Senate Subcommittees Begin Major Inquiry on White Collar Crime." **The Criminal Law Reporter,** 23, no. 13 (28 June 1978), pp. 2288-90.

928 "House Set to Get DP Crime Bill." **Computerworld,** 17, no. 43 (24 Oct. 1983), p. 5.

929 "How Blanket Licenses May Protect Software Developers." **Computer Law and Tax Report,** 5, no. 12 (July 1979), pp. 1-2.

930 "How Does the Computer Threaten Individual Privacy?" **Computer Law and Tax Report,** 4, no. 1 (Aug. 1977), p. 6.

931 "How Much Trouble Is Privacy?" **Computer Law and Tax Report,** 5, no. 5 (Dec. 1978), pp. 6-7.

932 "How Restrictions on Transnational Data Flow May Hurt Your Company." **Computer Law and Tax Report,** 5, no. 6 (Jan. 1979), pp. 1-2.

933 "How Secure Are Your Computers?" **Industry Week,** 186, no. 12 (22 Sept. 1975), pp. 40, 42-43.

934 "How Secure Your Site? Report Gives Equation." **Computerworld,** 16, no. 6 (8 Feb. 1982), pp. 91, 96.

935 "How to Bust a Bank with a $1,000 Computer Rig." **Business Week,** no. 2684 (20 Apr. 1981), pp. 90-91.

936 "How to Get Information Out of the Government." **Computer Law and Tax Report,** 4, no. 4 (Nov. 1977), pp. 1-3.

937 Howe, Charles L. "Coping with Computer Criminals." **Datamation,** 28, no. 1 (Jan. 1982), pp. 118+.

938 "How's Your Operations Security?" **Computer Law and Tax Report**, 6, no. 1 (Aug. 1979), pp. 2-3.

939 Hsia, David C. "Legislative History and Proposed Regulatory Implementation of the Electronic Fund Transfer Act." **University of San Francisco Law Review**, 13, no. 2 (Winter 1979), pp. 299-329.

940 Hubbert, James F. "Computer Personnel Frauds." **EDPACS**, 6, no. 9 (Mar. 1979), pp. 4-7.

941 Huckfield, Leslie. "Computers and Privacy." **The Parliamentarian**, 52, no. 3 (July 1971), pp. 181-86.

942 Huff, K. "Computers Can Be Robbed, Tricked or Sabotaged, Warns an Expert, and Their Power, If Abused, Could Cause Havoc." **People Weekly**, 20 (12 Sept. 1983), pp. 49-50.

943 Huntley, Steve. "Keyboard Bandits Who Steal Your Money." **U.S. News and World Report**, 93, no. 26 (27 Dec. 1982-3 Jan. 1983), pp. 68-69.

944 Hurley, Susan. "Colleges Fear Higher Degree of DP Abuse: Student Facing Charges." **Computerworld**, 16, no. 21 (24 May 1982), pp. 1, 8.

945 _____. "DEC Technicians Told of Security Trends." **Computerworld**, 16, no. 13 (29 Mar. 1982), p. 22.

946 Hurst, John. "Programs Seen Most Vulnerable to DP Privacy." **Computerworld**, 17, no. 48 (28 Nov. 1983), pp. SR 15-16.

947 Hyman, Warren H. "Larceny Enters the Electronic Age: The Problem of Detecting and Preventing Computer Crimes." **Gonzaga Law Review**, 18, no. 3 (1982-83), pp. 517-38.

948 "IBM Documents Say Accused Employees Familiar with Key Marketing Strategies." **Computerworld**, 16, no. 38 (20 Sept. 1982), p. 4.

949 "IBM's Security Outlined at Meet." **Computerworld**, 17, no. 46 (14 Nov. 1983), p. 17.

950 "IRS Treading on Thin Ice." **Computerworld**, 15, no. 47 (23 Nov. 1981), p. 30.

951 Iandiorio, Joseph S. "Protecting Computer Programs—The Conventional Forms of Protection Are Still Available." **Boston Bar Journal**, 16, no. 10 (Nov. 1972), pp. 25-27.

952 _____. "Protecting Software and Other Computer-Related Inventions and Innovation." **Boston Bar Journal**, 26, no. 5 (May 1982), pp. 22-26.

953 _____. "Which Wei Did They Go?" **Journal of the Patent Office Society**, 53, no. 11 (Nov. 1971), pp. 712-31.

954 "Ibis Countersues Burroughs, Seeks Damages to $85 Million." **Computerworld**, 16, no. 35 (30 Aug. 1982), p. 69.

955 "If Your System Doesn't Work—Remember The Green Monster." **Computer Law and Tax Report**, 5, no. 12 (July 1979), p. 2.

956 Immel, A. Richard. "Sabotage, Accidents, and Fraud Cause Woes for Computer Centers." **The Wall Street Journal**, 178 (22 Mar. 1971), p. 1, col. 6.

957 "Imposing Liability on Data Processing Services—Should California Choose Fraud or Warranty?" **Santa Clara Lawyer**, 13, no. 1 (Fall 1972), pp. 140-69.

958 "In re Johnston: New Output by the CCPA on the Patentability of Computer Software." **University of Pittsburgh Law Review**, 36, no. 3 (Spring 1975), pp. 739-55.

959 "In re Johnston: Patentability of Computer Software—The Battle Rages On." **Ohio Northern University Law Review**, 2, no. 4 (1975), pp. 782-87.

960 "Information Is a Thing of Value, Says Criminal Court." **Computer Law and Tax Report**, 6, no. 2 (Sept. 1979), pp. 3-5.

961 Ingraham, D.G. "DP Crime Bills: One Person's Trivia Is Another's Living." **Computerworld**, 18 (6 Aug. 1984), p. 42.

962 Ingraham, Donald G. "On Charging Computer Crime." **Computer/Law Journal**, 2, no. 2 (Spring 1980), pp. 429-39.

963 "Injunction Issued Against Selling Apple Doubles." **Computerworld**, 17, no. 20 (16 May 1983), p. 141.

964 "Inman on Role at MCC, National Security." **Computerworld**, 17, no. 21 (23 May 1983), pp. 15-16.

965 "Insurance Companies Offering Coverage for Computer Crime." **Journal of Commerce**, 352 (11 May 1982), p. 1A.

966 "Insuring Against Computer Foul-Ups." **Business Week**, no. 2755 (6 Sept. 1982), p. 66.

967 "Intellectual Property Protection for Computer Programs: Are Patents Now Obtainable?" **Catholic University Law Review**, 26, no. 4 (Summer 1977), pp. 835-51.

968 "The Internal Auditor and the Computer." **EDP Analyzer**, 13, no. 3 (Mar. 1975), pp. 1-13.

969 "International Copyright Law Applied to Computer Programs in the United States and France." **Loyola University of Chicago Law Journal**, 14, no. 1 (Fall 1982), pp. 105-38.

970 "International Legal Problems of Computer Communications: Automation of the Transnational Information Flow." **University of Toronto Law Journal**, 20 (1970), pp. 337-58.

971 "Intrusions Upon Informational Seclusion in the Computer Age." **The John Marshall Law Review**, 17, no. 3 (Summer 1984), pp. 831-48.

972 "Inventor Licenses Info Patents to IBM." **Computerworld**, 15, no. 48 (30 Nov. 1981) p. 84.

973 Irwin, Manley R. "Computers and Communications: Public Policy at the Crossroads." **Rutgers Journal of Computers and the Law**, 1970, no. 2 (Fall 1970), pp. 35-49.

974 "Is This the End or Just the Beginning of High-Technology Draft Registration?" **Computerworld**, 16, no. 20 (17 May 1982), p. 7.

975 "Is Your Computer Really Secure?" **Data System** (Aug. 1977), pp. 7-9.

976 "Israeli Tax Auditors Find Massive Fraud." **The Wall Street Journal**, 197, no. 27 (9 Feb. 1981), p. 20.

977 "It's Fine to Yell and Scream, but If You Don't Sue, You've Had It." **Computer Law and Tax Report**, 6, no. 2 (Sept. 1979), pp. 1-3.

978 Jacobs, Morton C. "Computer Technology (Hardware and Software): Some Legal Implications for Antitrust, Copyrights and Patents." **Rutgers Journal of Computers and the Law**, 1970, no. 2 (Fall 1970), pp. 50-69.

979 _____. "Patents for Software Inventions—The Supreme Court's Decision." **Jurimetrics Journal**, 13, no. 3 (Spring 1973), pp. 132-34.

980 Jacobson, Donald A. "Computer Software Theft Protection." **Bench & Bar of Minnesota**, 39, no. 3 (Dec. 1982), pp. 61-62.

981 Jennings, Marianne M. "Malfunction Liability Limitations in Computer Contracts—Who's Winning?" **Law/Technology**, 16, no. 1 (1st Quarter 1983), pp. 3-19.

982 Jetton, Julie Wilson. "Evra Corp. v. Swiss Bank Corp.: Consequential Damages for Bank Negligence in Wire Transfers." **Rutgers Computer & Technology Law Journal**, 9, no. 2 (1983), pp. 369-402.

983 Johnsen, Torkil C. "Observations on the Patentability of Computer Software." **International Review of Industrial Property and Copyright Law**, 2, no. 1 (1971), pp. 71-76.

984 Johnson, Bob. "Attendees Find Security Meet Topics Valuable." **Computerworld**, 16, no. 47 (22 Nov. 1982), p. 20.

985 _____. "Auditors Mount Campaign for DP Abuse Laws." **Computerworld**, 16, no. 23 (7 June 1982), p. 13.

986 _____. "Burroughs, User May Settle Suit." **Computerworld**, 16, no. 28 (12 July 1982), pp. 1, 6.

987 _____. "College Learns Lesson About Computer Crime."
Computerworld, 16, no. 8 (22 Feb. 1982), p. 23.

988 _____. "DP Crime to Snowball in '80s, Keynoter Warns."
Computerworld, 16, no. 17 (26 Apr. 1982), p. 10.

989 _____. "DP 'Hacking' Seen as Addiction to be Squelched."
Computerworld, 17, no. 16 (18 Apr. 1983), p. 32.

990 _____. "DP Security Exec Praises FBI and IBM; Terms
Industrial Espionage 'Fact of Life'." **Computerworld**, 16,
no. 26 (28 June 1982), p. 4.

991 _____. "DP Security Officers Urged to View Big Pic-
ture." **Computerworld**, 17, no. 14 (4 Apr. 1983), p. 13.

992 _____. "DP Teacher Charged in Funds Transfer Scam."
Computerworld, 16, no. 13 (29 Mar. 1982), p. 6.

993 _____. "The Fewer DP Laws, the Better, DP Execs
Say." **Computerworld**, 16, no. 45 (8 Nov. 1982), p. 7.

994 _____. "IACSS to Offer DP Security Certification
Exam." **Computerworld**, 17, no. 14 (4 Apr. 1983), p. 12.

995 _____. "Judge Rules Personal Use of Employer's Computer Legal." **Computerworld**, 16, no. 18 (3 May 1982),
pp. 1, 8.

996 _____. "Know Areas of Negotiation in Contract: Lawyer." **Computerworld**, 17, no. 14 (4 Apr. 1983), p. 37.

997 _____. "Lawyer Sees Trade Secrets Suits Escalating."
Computerworld, 16, no. 37 (13 Sept. 1982), p. 15.

998 _____. "Lawyer: Trade Secret Theft Hard to Prove."
Computerworld, 16, no. 44 (1 Nov. 1982), p. 80.

999 _____. "Legal Community at Odds Over Weg Decision."
Computerworld, 16, no. 19 (10 May 1982), p. 4.

1000 _____. "Liability Security Need Seen." **Computerworld**,
16, no. 49 (6 Dec. 1982), p. 83.

1001 _____. "Multinational Firms Warned on DP Security."
Computerworld, 17, no. 7 (14 Feb. 1983), p. 19.

1002 _____. "N.Y. Audit Finds Hospital DP Services Faulty."
Computerworld, 15, no. 41 (12 Oct. 1981), p. 19.

1003 _____. "N.Y. Bar Offers Alternative DP Crime Statute."
Computerworld, 16, no. 49 (6 Dec. 1982), p. 14.

1004 _____. "N.Y. Bar Subcommittee Rejects Two DP Crime
Bills." Computerworld, 16, no. 45 (8 Nov. 1982), p. 6.

1005 _____. "N.Y. Mayor Tightens Use of Municipal Computers." Computerworld, 15, no. 28 (13 July 1981), p. 22.

1006 _____. "Old Laws Affect New DP Industry: Attorney."
Computerworld, 16, no. 24 (14 June 1982), p. 14.

1007 _____. "Programmer Charged in Horse Breeding Scam."
Computerworld, 15, no. 28 (13 July 1981), p. 23.

1008 _____. "Record Crowds Test Security Aids at CSI Meet."
Computerworld, 16, no. 47 (22 Nov. 1982), p. 21.

1009 _____. "'Sabre' User Says American Tampering Possible." Computerworld, 16, no. 21 (24 May 1982), p. 6.

1010 _____. "Spies Seen Penetrating Corporate Centers."
Computerworld, 16, no. 22 (31 May 1982), p. 11.

1011 _____. "Swat Team Approach to DP Fraud Advocated."
Computerworld, 16, no. 4 (25 Jan. 1982), p. 29.

1012 _____. "Visa Installing System to Combat Fraud." Computerworld, 15, no. 37 (7 Sept. 1981), p. 19.

1013 Johnson, Maria Metzler. "An Update on EFTS." Rutgers
Journal of Computers and the Law, 6, no. 2 (1978), pp.
277-95.

1014 Johnston, R.E. "Halting the Hackers." Infosystems, 30, no.
12 (Dec. 1983), p. 62.

1015 Johnston, Ronald L. "Vendor Beware: The Copyright Laws
Require That You Exercise Caution." Computerworld,
16, no. 34 (23 Aug. 1982), pp. 59-60.

1016 "Joint Authors Hold Copyright." Computerworld, 16, no.
50 (13 Dec. 1982), p. 25.

1017 Jones, David C. "Computer Fraud Seen Misnomer: Human Element Must be Blamed." **National Underwriters Property Edition,** 81, no. 40 (8 Oct. 1977), p. 18.

1018 Jones, G. Hunter. "DP Error and Fraud—And What You Can Do About It." **Price Waterhouse Review,** 21, no. 2 (1976), pp. 3-11.

1019 Jordan, David E. "The Tortious Computer—When Does EDP Become Errant Data Processing?" **Computer Law Service,** 4, §5-1, art. 2 (1972), pp. 1-21.

1020 "Justice Seeks Dismissal in IBM Case." **Computerworld,** 17, no. 10 (7 Mar. 1983), p. 12.

1021 "Justice Study Addresses Computer Crime." **Computerworld,** 17, no. 19 (9 May 1983), p. 24.

1022 Karjala, Dennis S. "Lessons from the Computer Software Protection Debate in Japan." **Arizona State Law Journal,** 1984, no. 1 (1984), pp. 53-82.

1023 Katskee, Melvin R., and Ann L. Wright. "An Overview of the Legal Issues Confronting the Establishment of Electronic Funds Transfer Services." **Computer/Law Journal,** 2, no. 1 (Winter 1980), pp. 7-26.

1024 Kaul, Donald A. "And Now, State Protection of Intellectual Property?" **American Bar Association Journal,** 60 (Feb. 1974), pp. 198-202.

1025 Kayton, Irving. "Update of Legal Protection of Computer Software via Patents." **APLA Quarterly Journal,** 8, no. 3 (1980), pp. 273-78.

1026 Keefe, Arthur John, and Terry G. Mahn. "Protecting Software: Is It Worth All the Trouble?" **American Bar Association Journal,** 62 (July 1976), pp. 906-7.

1027 Keefe, Patricia. "Computer Crime Insurance Available—For a Price." **Computerworld,** 17, no. 44 (31 Oct. 1983), p. 20.

1028 _____. "Disaster Recovery Industry Burgeoning." **Computerworld,** 17, no. 38 (19 Sept. 1983), p. 73.

1029 _____. "Ex-DP Chiefs Plead Guilty to $1.3 Million Scam." **Computerworld**, 17, no. 28 (11 July 1983), p. 15.

1030 _____. "German DPer Charged with Stealing Tapes." **Computerworld**, 17, no. 32 (8 Aug. 1983), p. 17.

1031 _____. "Insurers Say 'Anti-Hacking' Policies Not Selling." **Computerworld**, 17, no. 44 (31 Oct. 1983), p. 21.

1032 _____. "Nine Charged in DP Fraud Suit." **Computerworld**, 17, no. 19 (9 May 1983), pp. 1, 4.

1033 _____. "Several Public Nets Dismiss Hacker Problem." **Computerworld**, 17, no. 37 (12 Sept. 1983), p. 13.

1034 _____. "Zilog Law Suit Charges NEC with Patent Infringement." **Computerworld**, 17, no. 14 (4 Apr. 1983), p. 99.

1035 Keliher, Michael J. "Computer Security and Privacy." **Vital Speeches of the Day**, 46, no. 21 (15 Aug. 1980), pp. 662–66.

1036 Kelly, Orr. "Pentagon Computers: How Vulnerable to Spies?" **U.S. News and World Report**, 95, no. 18 (31 Oct. 1983), pp. 36–37.

1037 Kelso, J. Clark and Alexandra Rebay. "Problems of Interpretation Under the 1980 Computer Amendment." **Santa Clara Law Review**, 23, no. 4 (1983), pp. 1001–35.

1038 Kennedy, Neal R. "A Look at Computer Crime—Oklahoma and Federal Law." **The Oklahoma Bar Journal**, 59, no. 49 (31 Dec. 1983), pp. 3263–74.

1039 Keplinger, Michael S. "Computer Intellectual Property Claims: Computer Software and Data Base Protection." **Washington University Law Quarterly**, 1977, no. 3 (Summer 1977), pp. 461–67.

1040 _____. "Computer Software—Its Nature and Its Protection." **Emory Law Journal**, 30 (1981), pp. 483–512.

1041 "Key-Punch Crooks." **Time**, 100, no. 26 (25 Dec. 1972), p. 69.

1042 King, Benjamin E., and Arthur G. Spence. "How to Tackle Computer Litigation." **Los Angeles Lawyer,** 3, no. 1 (Mar. 1980), pp. 34-38.

1043 Kirby, M.D. "The Computer, the Individual and the Law." **The Australian Law Journal,** 55, no. 7 (July 1981), pp. 443-57.

1044 _____. "Data Protection & Law Reform." **Computer Networks,** 3, no. 3 (June 1979), pp. 149-63.

1045 _____. "Developing International Rules to Protect Privacy." **Law and Computer Technology,** 12, no. 3 (3rd Quarter 1979), pp. 53-62.

1046 _____. "Eight Years to 1984: Privacy and Law Reform." **Rutgers Journal of Computers and the Law,** 5, no. 2 (1976), pp. 487-502.

1047 Kirchner, Jake. "Attorney: More Privacy Legislation Necessary." **Computerworld,** 17, no. 2 (10 Jan. 1983), p. 18.

1048 _____. "Bill Introduced in Senate to Study ID Systems in DP Age." **Computerworld,** 17, no. 32 (8 Aug. 1983), p. 23.

1049 _____. "COE Privacy Pact Threat to U.S. Downplayed." **Computerworld,** 17, no. 26 (27 June 1983), p. 13.

1050 _____. "CSC, Employees Found Innocent." **Computerworld,** 17, no. 24 (13 June 1983), pp. 141, 154.

1051 _____. "CSC, Justice Settle Fraud Charges in 11th Hour; CSC to Pay $2,950,000." **Computerworld,** 17, no. 28 (11 July 1983), p. 2.

1052 _____. "Charges of Airline DP 'Dirty Tricks' Probed." **Computerworld,** 16, no. 22 (31 May 1982), p. 5.

1053 _____. "China Seen Tapping U.S." **Computerworld,** 16, no. 30 (26 July 1982), pp. 1, 8.

1054 _____. "Computer Crime Legislation Resurfaces Briefly." **Computerworld,** 16, no. 40 (4 Oct. 1982), p. 19.

1055 _____. "Concerned House to Study Security Plan; Pentagon Draws Up Even Tougher One." **Computerworld,** 16, no. 10 (8 Mar. 1982), p. 2.

1056 _____. "Congress Expected to OK Driver Register." **Computerworld,** 16, no. 27 (5 July 1982), pp. 1, 6.

1057 _____. "Congress Urged to Address Federal DP Security." **Computerworld,** 17, no. 32 (8 Aug. 1983), p. 16.

1058 _____. "Congress Urged to Update Copyright Laws Soon." **Computerworld,** 17, no. 31 (1 Aug. 1983), p. 20.

1059 _____. "Court Date Set in Suit Over Prime Supermini." **Computerworld,** 17, no. 19 (9 May 1983), p. 4.

1060 _____. "DP Crime Bill Protecting Small Firms Introduced." **Computerworld,** 17, no. 24 (13 June 1983), p. 15.

1061 _____. "DP Crime Prevention Bill Gains Momentum in House." **Computerworld,** 17, no. 31 (1 Aug. 1983), p. 16.

1062 _____. "Data Accumulation Seen Devouring Liberties." **Computerworld,** 16, no. 18 (3 May 1982), p. 15.

1063 _____. "Dole Urges Halt to FBI Data Index." **Computerworld,** 15, no. 47 (23 Nov. 1981), pp. 1, 10.

1064 _____. "Efforts Urged to Keep High Tech from USSR." **Computerworld,** 16, no. 47 (22 Nov. 1982), p. 5.

1065 _____. "Encryption Endorsed as Way to End Hacking Plan." **Computerworld,** 17, no. 47 (21 Nov. 1983), p. 13.

1066 _____. "Explicit Policies Needed on EFT, OTA Report Warns." **Computerworld,** 16, no. 16 (19 Apr. 1982), p. 15.

1067 _____. "FBI Brings Up Surveillance System." **Computerworld,** 17, no. 21 (23 May 1983), p. 2.

1068 _____. "FBI Encouraged by Crime File Decentralization." **Computerworld,** 15, no. 45 (9 Nov. 1981), p. 9.

1069 _____. "Federal Systems Controls Found Inadequate." **Computerworld,** 17, no. 31 (1 Aug. 1983), p. 21.

1070 (Kirchner, Jake, cont.) "Free Trade v. Protectionism: Selling High Technology." **Computerworld**, 16/17, nos. 52/1 (27 Dec. 1982/3 Jan. 1983), pp. 59-62, 66.

1071 _____. "GAO: Government DP Security Deteriorating." **Computerworld**, 16, no. 20 (17 May 1982), p. 14.

1072 _____. "GTE Telenet Exec Calls for Anti-Hacker Law." **Computerworld**, 17, no. 47 (21 Nov. 1983), p. 12.

1073 _____. "Hackers Could Undermine Confidence in Federal Agencies, House Panel Told." **Computerworld**, 17, no. 43 (24 Oct. 1983), p. 4.

1074 _____. "Hackers Steal Legislator's Attention." **Computerworld**, 17, no. 37 (12 Sept. 1983), pp. 14-15.

1075 _____. "House Begins Hearings on Study Knocking Lack of U.S. Tech Policy." **Computerworld**, 17, no. 15 (11 Apr. 1983), pp. 105, 108.

1076 _____. "House Gets DP Crime Bill—Again." **Computerworld**, 15, no. 26 (29 June 1981), p. 2.

1077 _____. "House Passes Small Business DP Crime Bill." **Computerworld**, 17, no. 44 (31 Oct. 1983), p. 15.

1078 _____. "House to Act on Bill Embodying ID System." **Computerworld**, 16, no. 42 (18 Oct. 1982), p. 6.

1079 _____. "IRS Using Its Computers to Help Enforce Draft." **Computerworld**, 16, no. 34 (23 Aug. 1982), p. 5.

1080 _____. "Industry Spokesman Take Strong Exception to Bill to End Procurement Fraud." **Computerworld**, 15, no. 39 (28 Sept. 1981), p. 58.

1081 _____. "Justice Probes Six Japanese Firms for Chip Export Price Fixing." **Computerworld**, 16, no. 32 (9 Aug. 1982), p. 67.

1082 _____. "Legislation Easing Access to IRS Data Assailed." **Computerworld**, 15, no. 46 (16 Nov. 1981), p. 7.

1083 _____. "NSA Chief Pledges Open DP Security Center." **Computerworld**, 15, no. 38 (21 Sept. 1981), p. 13.

1084 _____. "National Driver Register Targeted for Extinction by Reagan Budget Cutters." **Computerworld**, 15, no. 26 (29 June 1981), p. 10.

1085 _____. "No DP Crime Law Again This Year." **Computerworld**, 17, no. 48 (28 Nov. 1983), pp. 1, 8.

1086 _____. "No Security Checks; Hospital Now Sorry." **Computerworld**, 16, no. 22 (31 May 1982), pp. 1, 7.

1087 _____. "Parker Eyes Paid Informers to Stem DP Crime." **Computerworld**, 15, no. 24 (15 June 1981), p. 20.

1088 _____. "Privacy—A History of Computer Matching in Federal Government." **Computerworld**, 15, no. 50 (14 Dec. 1981), pp. ID 1-3, 6-7, 10-11+.

1089 _____. "Privacy Coalition Seeks Congressional Support." **Computerworld**, 17, no. 14 (4 Apr. 1983), p. 17.

1090 _____. "Privacy Issues in 1984." **Computerworld**, 17/18, no. 52/1 (26 Dec. 1983/2 Jan. 1984), pp. 85-86.

1091 _____. "Privacy Plan Developed for Videotex." **Computerworld**, 17, no. 28 (11 July 1983), pp. 1, 4.

1092 _____. "Privacy Ranks High in Canadian Corners." **Computerworld**, 17, no. 40 (3 Oct. 1983), p. 8.

1093 _____. "Reagan Again Says No to National ID Cards." **Computerworld**, 15, no. 42 (19 Oct. 1981), p. 7.

1094 _____. "Reagan Delays Security Plan." **Computerworld**, 16, no. 9 (1 Mar. 1982), pp. 1-2.

1095 _____. "Reagan Fostering Support for OECD Policy." **Computerworld**, 15, no. 27 (6 July 1981), p. 7.

1096 _____. "Reagan Order Shows Secrecy Mania." **Computerworld**, 16, no. 15 (12 Apr. 1982), pp. 1, 8.

1097 _____. "Reagan Policy Paper on Trade Recognizes the Importance of High Technology and R & D." **Computerworld**, 15, no. 30 (27 July 1981), pp. 67-68.

1098 (Kirchner, Jake, cont.) "Reagan Raising Concerns Over Privacy with Revival of Broad DP Matching Plan." **Computerworld**, 15, no. 39 (28 Sept. 1981), p. 2.

1099 _____. "Report Lets Secret Service DP Off the Hook." **Computerworld**, 15, no. 36 (7 Sept. 1981), pp. 1, 6.

1100 _____. "Report Slams Administration's Privacy Record." **Computerworld**, 17, no. 47 (21 Nov. 1983), p. 15.

1101 _____. "SSA Defends DP System Before House Group." **Computerworld**, 15, no. 40 (5 Oct. 1981), p. 11.

1102 _____. "Second DP Fraud Bill Reaches House." **Computerworld**, 17, no. 41 (10 Oct. 1983), p. 13.

1103 _____. "Senate OK's Bill Embodying Worker ID System." **Computerworld**, 17, no. 22 (30 May 1983), p. 5.

1104 _____. "Senate Panel Criticizes Computer Matching." **Computerworld**, 17, no. 2 (10 Jan. 1983), pp. 17-18.

1105 _____. "Social Security Drafted in Hunt for Evaders." **Computerworld**, 16, no. 20 (17 May 1982), pp. 1, 7.

1106 _____. "Study Cites Lack of Hard Data on EFT Crime." **Computerworld**, 17, no. 29 (18 July 1983), p. 12.

1107 _____. "Study: Split Public, Private Information Roles." **Computerworld**, 15, no. 36 (7 Sept. 1981), p. 17.

1108 _____. "Study Warns Policymakers to Focus on DP Issues." **Computerworld**, 15, no. 45 (9 Nov. 1981), p. 37.

1109 _____. "Subcommittee Opposes Using IRS Files for Draft." **Computerworld**, 16, no. 32 (9 Aug. 1982), p. 8.

1110 _____. "Teenage Hacker Lectures House on DP Security." **Computerworld**, 17, no. 40 (3 Oct. 1983), pp. 1, 12.

1111 _____. "U.S. Chamber of Commerce Endorses Trade Bill." **Computerworld**, 17, no. 38 (19 Sept. 1983), p. 98.

1112 _____. "U.S. Firms, Trade Groups Back Privacy Rules." **Computerworld**, 15, no. 38 (21 Sept. 1981), p. 21.

1113 _____. "U.S. Privacy Efforts Well-Received by OECD."
Computerworld, 15, no. 47 (23 Nov. 1981), p. 23.

1114 _____. "U.S. Urged to Push International Privacy
Rules." Computerworld, 17, no. 26 (27 June 1983), p. 12.

1115 _____. "Ware Pins Hacking Liability on System Opera-
tor." Computerworld, 17, no. 44 (31 Oct. 1983), p. 19.

1116 _____. "You Can't Prevent a Tap: Experts." Computerworld, 16, no. 24 (14 June 1982), p. 26.

1117 Kling, Rob. "Computer Abuse and Computer Crime as
Organizational Activities." Computer/Law Journal, 2,
no. 2 (Spring 1980), pp. 403-27.

1118 _____. "EFTS Social and Technical Issues." Computer
Law Service, 5, §8-1, art. 3 (1977), pp. 1-19.

1119 Koenig, C. Frederick, III. "Software Copyright: The Conflict Within CONTU." Bulletin of the Copyright Society
of the U.S.A., 27, no. 5 (June 1980), pp. 340-78.

1120 Kolata, Gina. "Computer Break-Ins Fan Security Fears."
Science, 221, no. 4614 (2 Sept. 1983), pp. 930-31.

1121 _____. "Scheme to Foil Software Pirates." Science, 221,
no. 4617 (23 Sept. 1983), p. 1279.

1122 Kondos, George. "Criminal Records: Private Rights and
Public Need." Law and Computer Technology, 8, no. 6
(Dec. 1975), pp. 144-49.

1123 Kramer, Eugene H. "Computers Add New Dimensions to
Accountants' Legal Liability." Practical Accountant, 7,
no. 2 (Mar./Apr. 1974), pp. 46-47.

1124 Krieger, Michael M. "Current and Proposed Computer
Crime Legislation." Computer/Law Journal, 2, no. 3
(Summer 1980), pp. 721-71.

1125 Kudlinski, James R., Allen L. Raiken, and Raymond F.
Hodgdon. "Confidentiality of EFT Information." University of San Francisco Law Review, 13, no. 2 (Winter
1979), pp. 449-65.

1126 Laberis, Bill. "Anacomp Files Suit Against Former Employee." **Computerworld**, 16, no. 42 (18 Oct. 1982), p. 7.

1127 _____. "Consultant: Execs Need Help Against DP Crime." **Computerworld**, 15, no. 41 (12 Oct. 1981), p. 24.

1128 _____. "Florida Officials Put Lid on Food Stamp Fraud." **Computerworld**, 15, no. 31 (3 Aug. 1981), p. 14.

1129 _____. "For Second Time in Two Months, NCR Must Pay Damages to User." **Computerworld**, 17, no. 36 (5 Sept. 1983), pp. 1-2.

1130 _____. "Frugal State Pours Millions Down DP Drain." **Computerworld**, 15, no. 44 (2 Nov. 1981), pp. 1, 8.

1131 _____. "House Committee Among Those Examining Paradyne's SSA Pact." **Computerworld**, 17, no. 15 (11 Apr. 1983), pp. 105-106.

1132 _____. "IBM Adds, Drops Charges in Bridge Tech Case." **Computerworld**, 16, no. 48 (29 Nov. 1982), p. 6.

1133 _____. "Job Frustration Seen Incubator for DP Crime." **Computerworld**, 15, no. 41 (12 Oct. 1981), p. 25.

1134 _____. "Lewis Admits Guilt in Electronic Bank Heist." **Computerworld**, 15, no. 33 (17 Aug. 1981), p. 12.

1135 _____. "NCR Again Found Guilty of Breach of Contract." **Computerworld**, 17, no. 31 (1 Aug. 1983), pp. 1, 8.

1136 _____. "NCR Again Ordered to Pay User." **Computerworld**, 17, no. 41 (10 Oct. 1983), p. 2.

1137 _____. "O.P.M. Founders Sentenced in Fraud Case." **Computerworld**, 16/17, nos. 52/1 (27 Dec. 1982/3 Jan. 1983), pp. 107, 116.

1138 _____. "SEC Sues Paradyne Over Contract Fraud." **Computerworld**, 17, no. 14 (4 Apr. 1983), pp. 93, 97.

1139 _____. "Service Bureau Fined $25,000 for Performance." **Computerworld**, 15, no. 24 (15 June 1981), p. 9.

1140 _____. "South Dakota Breaks 370 Lease, Claims 1976
Contract Illegal." **Computerworld**, 15, no. 27 (6 July
1981), pp. 1, 6.

1141 _____. "System Ferrets Out Typewritten Forgeries."
Computerworld, 15, no. 37 (14 Sept. 1981), p. 27.

1142 _____. "User of HP 3000 Series 33 Files $5 Million
Suit Against Vendor." **Computerworld**, 16, no. 42 (18
Oct. 1982), pp. 1, 8.

1143 Labreche, Julianne. "Crime as a Terminal Problem."
Maclean's, 92, no. 8 (19 Feb. 1979), pp. 42, 44.

1144 Lahore, James. "Computers and the Law: The Protection
of Intellectual Property." **Federal Law Review**, 9, no. 1
(Mar. 1978), pp. 15-41.

1145 Land, Thomas. "Privacy vs. the Computer Revolution."
Computers and Automation, 22, no. 12 (Dec. 1973), pp.
14-16.

1146 Large, Peter. "Coping with Computer Crime." **World
Press Review**, 28, no. 7 (July 1981), p. 57.

1147 Lautsch, John C. "Computers, Communications and the
Wealth of Nations: Some Theoretical and Policy Con-
siderations About an Information Economy." **Computer/
Law Journal**, 4, no. 1 (Summer 1983), pp. 101-32.

1148 _____. "Digest and Analysis of State Legislation Relating to Computer Technology." **Jurimetrics Journal**,
20, no. 3 (Spring 1980), pp. 201-312.

1149 _____. "A Digest of State Legislation Relating to Computer Technology." **Jurimetrics Journal**, 17, no. 1 (Fall
1976), pp. 39-94.

1150 Laver, Ross. "Fighting Computer Pirates." **Maclean's**, 97,
no. 30 (23 July 1984), pp. 26-27.

1151 Lawlor, Reed C. "Benson and Beyond." **Computer Law
Service**, 3, §4-2, art. 3 (1974), pp. 1-29.

1152 _____. "A Proposal for Strong Protection of Computer

Programs Under the Copyright Law." **Jurimetrics Journal,** 20, no. 1 (Fall 1979), pp. 18-29.

1153 "Lawmakers Tackle Computer Crime." **Trial,** 20, no. 2 (Feb. 1984), p. 8.

1154 Leavitt, Don. "Program Patented as Apparatus." **Law and Computer Technology,** 7, no. 5 (Sept.-Oct. 1974), pp. 122-24.

1155 Lecht, Charles P. "Of Hacks and Hackers." **Computerworld,** 17, no. 44 (31 Oct. 1983), pp. 51, 54.

1156 Lee, Gerald W. "Auditor Concerns with EFTS: Too Many Risks for Comfort." **CA Magazine,** 115, no. 2 (Feb. 1982), pp. 36-41.

1157 "Legal Problems of Electronic Information Storage." **Tasmanian University Law Review,** 4, no. 1 (1971/1972), pp. 86-95.

1158 "Legal Protection of Software: A Matter of Monumental Insignificance?" **Computer Law and Tax Report,** 4, no. 7 (Feb. 1978), pp. 1-2.

1159 "Legislation Proposed Against Computer Fraud." **Credit World,** (Feb. 1978), p. 11.

1160 "Legislative Issues in Computer Crime." **Harvard Journal on Legislation,** 21, no. 1 (Winter 1984), pp. 239-54.

1161 Lennon, R.E. "Cryptography Architecture for Information Security." **IBM Systems Journal,** 17, no. 2 (1978), pp. 138-50.

1162 Letson, Laurence R. "Computer Program Protection in Three British Commonwealth Countries: What Can U.S. Learn?" **Idea,** 15, no. 2 (Summer 1971), pp. 304-21.

1163 Levary, Reuven R., and Karen K. Duke. "Some Aspects of Potential Disclosure of Confidential Computerized Legal Materials." **Computer/Law Journal,** 4, no. 1 (Summer 1983), pp. 159-69.

1164 Levin, Stephen E. "Security Possible in Communications

Networks." **Computerworld**, 17, no. 5 (31 Jan. 1983), pp. SR 6, 8, 10.

1165 Levy, Robert B. "Criminal Liability for Computer Offenses and the New Wisconsin Computer Crimes Act." **Wisconsin Bar Bulletin**, 56, no. 3 (Mar. 1983), pp. 21-23, 74-75.

1166 Lindsey, Robert. "Six Accused of Manipulating Credit Data Bank on Coast." **The New York Times**, 125 (3 Sept. 1976), p. 1, col. 6.

1167 Llewelyn, David and Harry Small. "Copyright in Computer Software: A Reply." **Solicitors' Journal**, 128, no. 21 (25 May 1984), pp. 358-60.

1168 Lobel, J. "Planning a Secure System." **Journal of Systems Management**, 27 (July 1976), pp. 14-19.

1169 Lobel, Jerome. "Security." **Computerworld OA**, 16, no. 39A (29 Sept. 1982), pp. 49-52.

1170 Lockhart, Thomas L., and John E. McGarry. "Patent Eligibility of Computer-Implemented Inventions in the Wake of Diehr." **Journal of Urban Law**, 59, no. 1 (Fall 1981), pp. 63-81.

1171 "Locking the Electronic File Cabinet." **Business Week**, no. 2761 (18 Oct. 1982), pp. 123-24.

1172 Lord, K.W., Jr. "Data Center Security: A Case for the Private Eye." **Infosystems**, 23 (Dec. 1976), pp. 30-31+.

1173 Lorr, Richard. "Copyright, Computers and Compulsory Licensing." **Rutgers Journal of Computers and the Law**, 5, no. 1 (1975), pp. 149-69.

1174 Lowry, Houston Putnam. "Does Computer Stored Data Constitute a Writing for the Purposes of the Statute of Frauds and the Statute of Wills?" **Rutgers Computer & Technology Law Journal**, 9, no. 1 (1982), pp. 93-107.

1175 Luccarelli, Peter A., Jr. "The Supremecy of Federal Copyright Law Over State Trade Secret Law for Copyrightable Computer Programs Marked with a Copyright Notice." **Computer/Law Journal**, 3 (1981), pp. 19-52.

1176 McCarthy, Michael P., and William C. Handorf. "Electronic Data Processing Audits and the Insured Sand L." **The Federal Home Loan Bank Board Journal,** 11, no. 5 (May 1978), pp. 18-21.

1177 MacDonald, Malcolm E. "Confidentiality and Security of Computerized Records." **Juvenile Justice,** 24, no. 4 (Feb. 1974), pp. 42-48.

1178 McFarlane, Gavin. "Legal Protection of Computer Programs." **Journal of Business Law,** 1970 (July 1970), pp. 204-8.

1179 MacGrady, Glenn J. "Protection of Computer Software— An Update and Practical Synthesis." **Houston Law Review,** 20, no. 4 (July 1983), pp. 1033-82.

1180 McGuire, Richard P. "The Information Age: An Introduction to Transborder Data Flow." **Jurimetrics Journal,** 20, no. 1 (Fall 1979), pp. 1-7.

1181 McKenzie, Evan. "Computer Programs and Copyright Law: The Object Code Controversy." **San Fernando Valley Law Review,** 11 (1983), pp. 1-20.

1182 Madden, Thomas J., and Helen S. Lessin. "Privacy: A Case for Accurate and Complete Criminal History Records." **Villanova Law Review,** 22, no. 6 (Oct. 1977), pp. 1191-1204.

1183 Maggs, Peter B. "Computer Programs as the Object of Intellectual Property in the United States of America." **The American Journal of Comparative Law,** 30 (1982), pp. 251-73.

1184 _____. "Some Problems of Legal Protection of Programs for Microcomputer Control Systems." **University of Illinois Law Forum,** 1979, no. 2 (1979), pp. 453-68.

1185 "Magnusun Secrets Case Goes to Closed Session." **Computerworld,** 17, no. 35 (29 Aug. 1983), p. 69.

1186 Mair, William, et al. "Computer Control and Audit: A Necessity." **Computers and People,** 25, no. 11 (Nov. 1976), pp. 18-21.

1187 Maki, Linda J., and John W. Jerak. "EFTS: Living in a
     Legal House of Cards." **Commercial Law Journal**, 84,
     no. 2 (Feb. 1979), pp. 49-62.

1188 "The Making of a Hacker." **Newsweek**, 102, no. 10 (5 Sept.
     1983), p. 44.

1189 Malik, Rex. "British M15 Systems Spark Privacy Ques-
     tions." **Computerworld**, 16, no. 14 (5 Apr. 1982), p. 28.

1190 _____, Michael Blee, and Hedley Voysey. "A Program
     for Computer Crime." **Data Systems**, 15, no. 8 (Oct.
     1974), pp. 10-12.

1191 Mandell, Mel. "Theft at Timesharing Outfit Poses Dis-
     turbing Threat." **Computer Decisions**, 13, no. 9 (Sept.
     1981), p. 8.

1192 Mano, D. Keith. "Computer Crime." **National Review**, 36,
     no. 14 (27 July 1984), pp. 51-2.

1193 Mantle, Ray A. "Trade Secret and Copyright Protection
     of Computer Software." **Computer/Law Journal**, 4, no.
     4 (Spring 1984), pp. 669-94.

1194 Marbach, W.D. "Beware: Hackers at Play." **Newsweek**,
     102 (5 Sept. 1983), pp. 42-46, 48.

1195 _____. "New Wave Computer Crime." **Newsweek**, 102
     (29 Aug. 1983), p. 45.

1196 Marbach, William D. "Cracking Down on Hackers." **News-
     week**, 102 (24 Oct. 1983), p. 34.

1197 Marcellino, James J., and Dexter L. Kenfield. "Legisla-
     tive Developments in High-Tech." **Boston Bar Journal**,
     28, no. 2 (Mar./Apr. 1984), pp. 19-23.

1198 Marcus, Michael. "Management Concerns in the '80s."
     Computerworld, 15, no. 41 (12 Oct. 1981), pp. ID 45-48.

1199 Markoski, Joseph P. "Telecommunications Regulations as
     Barriers to the Transborder Flow of Information." **Cor-
     nell International Law Journal**, 14 (1981), pp. 287-331.

1200 Marsh, R. "Making Data More Secure." **Datamation**, 22 (Oct. 1976), pp. 67-69.

1201 "Mass. Crime Bill Classifies Electronic Data as Property." **Computerworld**, 17, no. 19 (9 May 1983), p. 4.

1202 Masuda, Yoneji. "Privacy in the Future Information Society." **Computer Networks**, 3, no. 3 (June 1979), pp. 164-70.

1203 Matek, Michael S. "Limiting Liability in Personal Computer Equipment Contracts." **Commercial Law Journal**, 88, no. 9 (Nov. 1983), pp. 562-68.

1204 Mathew, Paul A. "Architects, Engineers, Computer Product and the Law: A Matter of Anticipation." **Computer/ Law Journal**, 3 (Spring 1982), pp. 337-83.

1205 Mathias, Charles, Jr. "Statement Before Senate Subcommittee on Constitutional Rights." **Trial**, 7, no. 2 (Mar.-Apr. 1971), p. 23.

1206 Mayer, Allan J. "The Computer Bandits." **Newsweek**, 88, no. 6 (9 Aug. 1976), pp. 58, 61.

1207 "The Medium Is the Message: Apple Computer, Inc. v. Franklin Computer Corporation." **University of San Francisco Law Review**, 18, no. 2 (Winter 1984), pp. 351-69.

1208 Medlock, V. Bryan. "Computer Program Protection. V. Which Type of Protection for Computer Programs Should Originators Seek--Patents, Copyrights, Trade Secrets or Combinations of These?" **Texas Bar Journal**, 34, no. 1 (Jan. 1971), pp. 59-60.

1209 Meissner, Paul. "Computers: A Seeing-Eye Watching You." **Science Digest**, 81, no. 6 (June 1977), pp. 64-67.

1210 _____. "Preventing Unauthorized Use of Systems." **Data Processing**, 19 (July/Aug. 1977), pp. 42-43.

1211 Menkus, Belden. "Computer Crooks May Be Robbing Your Bank Blind." **The Bankers Magazine**, 162, no. 3 (May-June 1979), pp. 35-37.

1212 _____. "Computer Security Needs a Common Sense

Approach." **Administrative Management,** 34, no. 3
(Mar. 1973), pp. 28-29, 42-43.

1213 Meyer, Eugene L. "Four Indicted in $500,000 Fraud by
Computer from Union's Funds." **The Washington Post,**
(16 Dec. 1976), sec. C, p. 1, col. 2.

1214 "Microcomputer Emulation: Protecting Manufacturers
from Computer Copying." **Suffolk University Law Review,** 17, no. 3 (Fall 1983), pp. 656-86.

1215 "Microkid Raids—The FBI Cracks Down." **Time,** 122 (24
Oct. 1983), p. 59.

1216 "Micropro Files Suit Against United Computer." **Computerworld,** 17, no. 27 (4 July 1983), p. 55.

1217 Milde, Karl F., Jr. "Life after Diamond v. Diehr: The
CCPA Speaks Out on the Patentability of Computer-
Related Subject Matter." **Journal of the Patent Office
Society,** 64, no. 8 (Aug. 1982), pp. 434-56.

1218 Milgrim, Roger M. "Software, Carfare and Benson." **Jurimetrics Journal,** 13, no. 4 (Summer 1973), pp. 240-47.

1219 Miller, Arthur R. "Computers, Data Banks and Individual
Privacy: An Overview." **Columbia Human Rights Law
Review,** 4, no. 1 (Winter 1972), pp. 1-12.

1220 Miller, Richard I. "The CONTU Software Protection Survey." **Jurimetrics Journal,** 18, no. 4 (Summer 1978), pp.
354-68.

1221 _____. "Computer v. Personal Dignity." **Trial,** 7, no. 2
(Mar.-Apr. 1971), pp. 26-27.

1222 Milligan, R.H. "Management Guide to Computer Protection." **Journal of Systems Management,** 27 (Nov. 1976),
pp. 14-18.

1223 "Milwaukee Discovers 'War Gamesmanship'." **Newsweek,**
102 (22 Aug. 1983), p. 22.

1224 "Misappropriation of Computer Services: The Need to
Enforce Civil Liability." **Computer/Law Journal,** 4, no.
2 (Fall 1983), pp. 401-20.

1225 "Mitsubishi Pleads Innocent." **Computerworld**, 16, no. 38 (20 Sept. 1982), p. 8.

1226 "Model Provisions on the Protection of Computer Software." **Law and Computer Technology**, 11, no. 1 (1st Quarter 1978), pp. 2-27.

1227 Moorhead, William S. "Limiting Liability in Electronic Data Processing Service Contracts." **Rutgers Journal of Computers and the Law**, 4, no. 1 (1974), pp. 141-62.

1228 "Morality in the Computer Classroom." **Datamation**, 28, no. 12 (Nov. 1982), pp. 222, 224.

1229 Mortimer, Harold E. "Current Legal Problems Facing Commercial Banks Participating in Electronic Funds Transfer Systems." **Banking Law Journal**, 95, no. 2 (Feb. 1978), pp. 116-42.

1230 _____, and Fairfax Leary, Jr. "Electronic Funds Transfers." **The Business Lawyer**, 33 (Feb. 1978), pp. 947-64.

1231 Moscove, Stephen A. "Is Computer Fraud a Fact of Business Life?" **The National Public Accountant**, 23, no. 8 (Aug. 1978), pp. 16-19, 22.

1232 Moskowitz, Nelson. "The Metamorphosis of Software-Related Invention Patentability." **Computer/Law Journal**, 3 (Spring 1982), pp. 273-336.

1233 "Motives for Theft." **Datamation**, 26, no. 9 (Sept. 1980), pp. 82, 84.

1234 "Multiuser Systems Need Fail-Safe Data Security." **Computerworld**, 17, no. 13 (28 Mar. 1983), p. SR11.

1235 Murphy, C. Westbrook, and Ford Barrett. "Legal Problems of Applying Electronic Funds Techniques to Retail Banking." **Jurimetrics Journal**, 17, no. 1 (Fall 1976), pp. 111-23.

1236 Murray, John. "Contingency Planning." **Computerworld**, 16, no. 19 (10 May 1982), pp. ID 35-40, 42, 44.

1237 Myers, David. "Hacker Debate Continues at Security Conference." **Computerworld**, 17, no. 46 (14 Nov. 1983), pp. 17-18.

1238 Myers, E. "Computer Criminals Beware!" **Datamation,** 21 (Dec. 1975), pp. 105+.

1239 _____. "Computer Security: Each Case Is Different." **Datamation,** 21 (Apr. 1975), pp. 107-109.

1240 _____. "Security—The Only Means to Privacy." **Datamation,** 23 (May 1977), pp. 240-242.

1241 Myers, Edith. "Pirates on the Boards." **Datamation,** 30, no. 6 (1 May 1984), pp. 61, 64.

1242 _____. "Privacy: A Political Issue." **Datamation,** 24, no. 5 (May 1978), pp. 261-63.

1243 Mylott, Thomas R., III. "Let the Buyer Beware: Legal Contracts." **Computerworld OA,** 16, no. 25A (23 June 1982), pp. 21-22.

1244 _____. "Users Urged to Agree with Vendor on Issues Before Buying Software." **Computerworld,** 16, no. 26 (28 June 1982), p. SR 12.

1245 "NCL Data Head Pleads Innocent in Hitachi Case." **Computerworld,** 17, no. 19 (9 May 1983), p. 4.

1246 "The Nagging Feeling of Undetected Fraud." **U.S. News and World Report,** 83, no. 25 (19 Dec. 1977), p. 42.

1247 "Negligence: Liability for Defective Software." **Oklahoma Law Review,** 33, no. 4 (Fall 1980), pp. 848-55.

1248 Nellis, Joseph L. "Computer Law Lags Behind Technology." **Data Management,** 20, no. 8 (Aug. 1982), pp. 14-15.

1249 Neville, Haig. "Computer 'Capers' Herald New Crime Wave of Embezzlement." **National Underwriter, Property and Casualty Ins. Ed.,** 75, no. 34 (20 Aug. 1971), pp. 1, 12-3.

1250 Neville, Haig G. "Computers Aid the Button-Down Crook." **National Underwriters Property Edition,** 78, no. 3 (18 Jan. 1974), p. 28.

1251 "New Jersey Court Balances Interests, User Awarded $120,000." **Computer Law and Tax Report,** 6, no. 7 (Feb. 1980), pp. 2-4.

1252 "New Law Sets Rules for Electronic Banking." **Consumer Reports,** 44, no. 2 (Feb. 1979), p. 65.

1253 "New Protections for Privacy in Australia." **Law/Technology,** 13, no. 4 (4th Quarter 1980), pp. 1-43.

1254 "New Technoloday (sic) and the Law: An Australian Perspective." **Law/Technology,** 14, no. 1 (1st Quarter 1981), pp. 1-48.

1255 "A New Way to STK Up Banks." **Time,** 115, no. 16 (21 Apr. 1980), p. 76.

1256 Niblett, Bryan. "Computer Security and the Law." **Computer Law Service,** 5, §9-2.2, art. 1 (1974), pp. 1-7.

1257 _____. "Copyright Aspects of Legal Databases." **Jurimetrics Journal,** 20, no. 1 (Fall 1979), pp. 30-40.

1258 Nicholson, Tom, and Jeff B. Copeland. "The Great Computer Heist." **Newsweek,** 92, no. 21 (20 Nov. 1978), pp. 99-100.

1259 Nimtz, R.O. "Diamond v. Diehr: A Turning Point." **Rutgers Journal of Computers, Technology and the Law,** 8 (1981), pp. 267-71.

1260 Nimtz, Robert O. "Development of the Law of Computer Software." **Computer Law Service,** 3, §4-1, art. 6 (1980), pp. 1-22.

1261 _____. "Development of the Law of Computer Software Protection." **Journal of the Patent Office Society,** 61, no. 1 (Jan. 1979), pp. 3-43.

1262 _____. "The Patentability of Computer Programs." **Rutgers Journal of Computers and the Law,** 1970, no. 1 (Spring 1970), pp. 38-49.

1263 Nolan, James. "FBI Agent Accountants Intensify Campaign Against 'White Collar' Crime." **Journal of Accountancy,** 138, no. 4 (Oct. 1974), pp. 26, 28, 30.

1264 Norman, A. "Computer Frauds—Are They a Manageable Risk?" **Accountancy,** 87 (Oct. 1976), pp. 78-9+.

1265 Norman, A.R.D. "Computer Fraud—The Villain's View of
the Opportunities." **Electronics and Power,** 24, no. 11
(Nov.-Dec. 1978), pp. 824-26.

1266 Norris, Richard H., III. "Legal Background of a Shared
EFT Network." **The Business Lawyer,** 34, no. 2 (Jan.
1979), pp. 527-36.

1267 "Nova Scotia Enacts Privacy Act." **Computer Law and
Tax Report,** 4, no. 8 (Mar. 1978), p. 7.

1268 Novick, Mitchell P., and Helene Wallenstein. "The Algorithm and Computer Software Patentability: A Scientific View of a Legal Problem." **Rutgers Journal of
Computers, Technology and the Law,** 7, no. 2 (1980),
pp. 313-41.

1269 Novotny, Eric J. "Transborder Data Flow Regulation:
Technical Issues of Legal Concern." **Computer/Law
Journal,** 3 (Winter 1982), pp. 105-24.

1270 "Now Is Time to Implement Communications Security."
ABA Banking Journal, 73, no. 7 (July 1981), pp. 54-55,
57, 59-60.

1271 Nycum, Susan. "Liability for Malfunction of a Computer
Program." **Rutgers Journal of Computers, Technology,
and the Law,** 7, no. 1 (1979), pp. 1-22.

1272 Nycum, Susan H., and William A. Lowell. "Common Law
and Statutory Liability for Inaccurate Computer-Based
Data." **Emory Law Journal,** 30, no. 2 (1981), pp. 445-81.

1273 _____, Dexter L. Kenfield, and Margaret A. Keenan.
"Debugging Software Escrow: Will It Work When You
Need It?" **Computer/Law Journal,** 4, no. 3 (Winter 1984),
pp. 441-63.

1274 Nycum, Susan Hubbell. "Computer Abuses Raise New Legal
Problems." **American Bar Association Journal,** 61 (Apr.
1975), pp. 444-48.

1275 _____. "Computer Crime—A Comment." **Computer/Law
Journal,** 2, no. 2 (Spring 1980), pp. XV-XVI.

1276 _____. "The Criminal Law Aspects of Computer A-
buse." **Rutgers Journal of Computers and the Law**, 5,
no. 2 (1976), pp. 271-322.

1277 _____. "Legal Problems of Computer Abuse." **Washington University Law Quarterly**, 1977, no. 3 (Summer
1977), pp. 527-36.

1278 _____. "Legal Protection for Computer Programs."
Computer/Law Journal, 1, no. 1 (Spring 1978), pp. 1-83.

1279 _____. "Security for Electronic Funds Transfer System."
University of Pittsburgh Law Review, 37, no. 4 (Summer
1976), pp. 709-24.

1280 "OMB Proposes Security Rules." **Computer Law and Tax
Report**, 4, no. 4 (Nov. 1977), p. 5.

1281 "OS/MVT Flunks Privacy Test." **Computer Law and Tax
Report**, 3, no. 10 (May 1977), pp. 1-2.

1282 Oberman, Michael S. "Copyright Protection for Computer-
Produced Directories." **ASCAP Copyright Law Symposium**, 22 (1977), pp. 1-52.

1283 "Object Program Held Not Copyrightable; No Protection
for ROMs?" **Computer Law and Tax Report**, 6, no. 5
(Dec. 1979), pp. 4-6.

1284 O'Brien, David M. "Privacy and the Right of Access: Purposes and Paradoxes of Information Control." **Administrative Law Review**, 30, no. 1 (Winter 1978), pp. 45-92.

1285 O'Connor, James. E. "Computer Professionals: The Need
for State Licensing." **Jurimetrics Journal**, 18, no. 3
(Spring 1978), pp. 256-67.

1286 Ohle, Mary Ann, and David Berreby. "A Grave Development on the Computer Front." **The National Law Journal**, 4, no. 33 (26 Apr. 1982), p. 47.

1287 Oler, Harriet Lee. "Statutory Copyright Protection for
Electronic Digital Computer Programs: Administrative
Considerations. Part One." **Law and Computer Tech-
nology**, 7, no. 4 (July-Aug. 1974), pp. 96-116.

1288 _____. "Statutory Copyright Protection for Electronic
Digital Computer Programs: Administrative Considerations. Part Two." **Law and Computer Technology,** 7,
no. 5 (Sept.-Oct. 1974), pp. 118-22.

1289 Oliver, Gary. "Get Promises on Paper Before Buying System." **Computerworld,** 16, no. 35 (30 Aug. 1982), p. SR21.

1290 "On Diamond v. Diehr and Lutton." **Idea,** 22, no. 2 (Spring
1981), pp. 104-12.

1291 "On-Line Theft Via Personal Computer." **EDPACS,** 6, no.
6 (Dec. 1978), p. 14.

1292 "On the Coast-to-Coast Trial of Equity Funding." **Business
Week,** no. 2276 (21 Apr. 1973), pp. 68, 70, 72.

1293 "On the Software Patent Front." **Computer Law and Tax
Report,** 3, no. 12 (July 1977), p. 3.

1294 "Once Again—Get It in Writing." **Computer Law and Tax
Report,** 5, no. 9 (Apr. 1979), pp. 5-6.

1295 Orr, Kenneth T. "Data Security and Privacy: Phase Two."
Infosystems, 23, no. 2 (Feb. 1976), pp. 34-35.

1296 "Outwitting 2 Bit Thieves and Arresting Computer Crime."
Data Communications, 12 (Nov. 1982), p. 117.

1297 Oxman, John Craig. "Intellectual Property Protection Integrated Circuit Masks." **Jurimetrics Journal,** 20, no. 4
(Summer 1980), pp. 405-60.

1298 Pagenberg, Birgett A. "Patentability of Computer Programs on the National and International Level." **International Review of Industrial Property and Copyright
Law,** 5, no. 1 (1974), pp. 1-43.

1299 Painter, Michael A. "Recent Developments in the Protec-
tion of Computer Programs Under the Patent System."
Journal of the Beverly Hills Bar Association, 5, no. 5
(Nov.-Dec. 1971), pp. 32-38.

1300 Palme, J. "Software Security." **Datamation,** 20 (Jan. 1974),
pp. 51-55.

1301 Pantages, Angeline. "The Price of Protection." **Datamation,** 22, no. 3 (Mar. 1976), pp. 141, 144.

1302 Parker. "What to Do to Keep Light Fingers Off a Bank's Computer." **Banking,** 65 (June 1973), p. 34.

1303 Parker, Donn B. "The Antisocial Use of Computers." **Computers and Automation,** 21, no. 8 (Aug. 1982), pp. 22-24.

1304 _____. "Computer Abuse Research Update." **Computer/ Law Journal,** 2, no. 2 (Spring 1980), pp. 329-52.

1305 _____. "Computer Crimes." **Office,** 78 (Aug. 1973), pp. 43-47.

1306 _____. "Computer Systems Protection: Testimony Before the U.S. Senate Committee." **Computers and People,** 27, no. 10 (Oct. 1978), pp. 7-12.

1307 _____. "Ethical DP Behavior Requires Action Plan." **Computerworld,** 16, no. 33 (16 Aug. 1982), pp. 39, 47.

1308 _____. "The Increasingly Binary Nature of Crime." **The New York Times,** 125 (11 July 1976), sec. F, p. 12, col. 2.

1309 _____. "The Round-Down Fraud." **The Bankers Magazine,** 160, no. 2 (Spring 1977), pp. 28-30.

1310 Parry, James. "Computer Theft: You May Be the Last to Know." **Canadian Business,** 49 (May 1976), pp. 63-64+.

1311 Parsons, Carole. "Computers and the International Flow of Information." **Computer Networks,** 3, no. 3 (June 1979), pp. 171-73.

1312 "Passwords." **The New York Times,** 130 (16 Aug. 1981), p. F21.

1313 "Patent Issue Called a Matter for Congress." **Electronics,** 51, no. 14 (6 July 1978), pp. 46+.

1314 "Patent Law—Computer Programs for Processing Data with a Digital Computer Cannot Be Patented Under Present United States Laws." **Loyola University Law Journal,** 4, no. 2 (Summer 1973), pp. 560-78.

1315 "Patent Law--Computer Programs--Unpatentable Mental
     Process--Gottschalk v. Benson." **Boston College Indus-
     trial and Commercial Law Review,** 14, no. 5 (May 1973),
     pp. 1051-71.

1316 "Patent Law: Patentability of a Process That Includes a
     Programmed Digital Computer: The Court Invents a
     New Standard." **University of Dayton Law Review,** 7,
     no. 1 (Fall 1981), pp. 157-68.

1317 "Patent Law--Patentability of Computer Programs--A
     Computerized Procedure That Has a Mathematical For-
     mula as Its Only Feature Is Not Patentable Subject Mat-
     ter." **University of Detroit Journal of Urban Law,** 56,
     no. 1 (Fall 1978), pp. 289-304.

1318 "Patent Law--Patentable Subject Matter--Computer
     Software--Parker v. Flook." **New York Law School Law
     Review,** 24, no. 4 (1979), pp. 975-84.

1319 "Patent Law--Patentable Subject Matter--Manufacturing
     Process Which Includes Use of Mathematical Formula
     and Computer Program Constitutes Patentable Subject
     Matter." **St. Mary's Law Journal,** 13, no. 2 (1981), pp.
     420-30.

1320 "Patent Law--Process Claim Involving Computer Program
     Meets Statutory Subject Matter Requirements." **Tulane
     Law Review,** 56, no. 2 (Feb. 1982), pp. 785-803.

1321 "Patent Law--Subject Matter Patentability--Computers
     and Mathematical Formulas." **Tennessee Law Review,**
     48, no. 4 (Summer 1981), pp. 1042-66.

1322 "Patent Law--Subject-Matter Patentability--Process
     Patents--The Patentability of Computer Software."
     Wisconsin Law Review, 1979, no. 3 (1979), pp. 867-95.

1323 "Patent Law--The Next-to-Last Step to Software Patent-
     ability?--Diamond v. Diehr, 450 U.S. 175 (1981)." **Camp-
     bell Law Review,** 4, no. 1 (Fall 1981), pp. 219-37.

1324 "Patentability of Computer Programs." **Baylor Law Re-
     view,** 34, no. 1 (Winter 1982), pp. 125-41.

1325 "Patentability of Computer Programs." **University of Miami Law Review**, 27, nos. 3-4 (Spring-Summer 1973), pp. 494-504.

1326 "Patentability of Computer Software: The Nonobviousness Issue." **Iowa Law Review**, 62, no. 2 (Dec. 1976), pp. 615-35.

1327 "Patentability of Software Technology." **Northern Illinois University Law Review**, 2 (Spring 1982), pp. 471-87.

1328 "Patentability: Piecing Together the Computer Software Patent Puzzle." **Saint Louis University Law Journal**, 19, no. 3 (Spring 1975), pp. 351-74.

1329 "Patenting Inventions That Embody Computer Programs As Trade Secrets." **Washington Law Review**, 59, no. 3 (1984), pp. 601-15.

1330 "Patents and Computer Programs—The Supreme Court Makes a Decision." **Kentucky Law Journal**, 62, no. 1 (1973-74), pp. 533-56.

1331 "Patents for Software Inventions—The Supreme Court's Decision." **Journal of the Patent Office Society**, 55, no. 1 (Jan. 1973), pp. 59-61.

1332 "Patents, Mathematics and Computer Software Bauer-Mengelberg, Parker v. Flook: A Formula to Cause Alarm." **Idea**, 21, no. 4 (1980), pp. 189-92.

1333 "Patents—Statutory Subject Matter Under 35 U.S.C. §101—Processes—Mathematical Formulae—Computer Programs—If a Patent Application Claims a Process Which Transforms or Reduces an Article to a Different State or Thing, The Process Is Statutory Subject Matter Under 35 U.S.C. §101, Not Withstanding the Fact That a Computer Program Embodying a Mathematical Formula Is One Element of the Process.—Diamond v. Diehr, 101 S. Ct. 1048 (1981)." **University of Cincinnati Law Review**, 50, no. 3 (1981), pp. 645-63.

1334 "Patents: U.S. Supreme Court to Review Flook." **Computer Law and Tax Report**, 4, no. 7 (Feb. 1978), pp. 2-3.

1335 Patrick, P. Howard. "Privacy Restrictions on Transnational Data Flows: A Comparison of the Council of Europe Draft Convention and OECD Guidelines." **Jurimetrics Journal,** 21, no. 4 (Summer 1981), pp. 405-20.

1336 Patrick, Robert L."Auditing and DP: Redressing the Relationship." **Datamation,** 24, no. 12 (15 Nov. 1978), pp. 139-40, 144.

1337 Paul, Lois. "Attorney Outlines Software Contract Procedures." **Computerworld,** 16, no. 13 (29 Mar. 1982), p. 19.

1338 _____. "Billion-Dollar Bank Makes Change in Security Setup." **Computerworld,** 15, no. 41 (12 Oct. 1981), p. 77.

1339 _____. "Con Claims Success Felled Prison DP Bureau." **Computerworld,** 16, no. 11 (15 Mar. 1982), p. 5.

1340 _____. "DP Scam Nets Over $4 Million; Six Indicted." **Computerworld,** 15, no. 24 (15 June 1981), pp. 1, 6.

1341 _____. "Exec Warns Computer Crime Already Here." **Computerworld,** 15, no. 27 (6 July 1981), p. 25.

1342 _____. "Farrell: 'Jesse James' Rides on in '80s." **Computerworld,** 15, no. 38 (21 Sept. 1981), pp. 25-26.

1343 _____. "Four Proposed Changes to Copyright Act Aired." **Computerworld,** 16, no. 33 (16 Aug. 1982), p. 15.

1344 _____. "Holder of Canceled Contract Sues." **Computerworld,** 15, no. 29 (20 July 1981), p. 14.

1345 _____. "IBMer Puts Responsibility for Security on User." **Computerworld,** 15, no. 39 (28 Sept. 1981), p. 15.

1346 _____. "'If It Is Not in the Contract, Then It Is Not in the Deal' Lawyer Reminds Licensers." **Computerworld,** 16, no. 13 (29 Mar. 1982), p. 17.

1347 _____. "Investment Groups File Fraud Suit Against Broker." **Computerworld,** 15, no. 27 (6 July 1981), p. 10.

1348 _____. "Moffat: Management Unaware of DP Security Vulnerabilities." **Computerworld,** 15, no. 38 (21 Sept. 1981), p. 24.

1349 _____. "Software Copyright Suit Settled Out of Court by Two DP Vendors." **Computerworld,** 16, no. 27 (5 July 1982), pp. 71, 79.

1350 _____. "Software Firms Unite to Fight Theft." **Computerworld,** 15, no. 26 (29 June 1981), pp. 63, 70.

1351 _____. "Vendor Tags Hardware to Protect Code." **Computerworld,** 17, no. 15 (11 Apr. 1983), pp. 53, 56.

1352 _____. "White-Collar DP Crime Seen Climbing in '80s." **Computerworld,** 16, no. 4 (25 Jan. 1982), p. 12.

1353 Peck. "Data Processing Safeguards." **Journal of Systems Management,** 23 (Oct. 1972), p. 11.

1354 Peltu, Malcolm. "The Rise and Rise of Computer Crime." **International Management,** 34, no. 7 (July 1979), pp. 44-48.

1355 Perle, E. Gabriel. "Copyright and New Technology." **Bulletin of the Copyright Society of the U.S.A.,** 25, no. 3 (Feb. 1978), pp. 250-54.

1356 Perry, William E. "Who's in Charge, You or Your Computer?" **Computer Decisions,** 10, no. 2 (Feb. 1978), pp. 38-39, 41.

1357 "Personal Data System Judged Unconstitutional." **Computer Decisions,** 10, no. 4 (Apr. 1978), p. 6.

1358 Peterson, Bill. "Convicted Computer Expert Seeks Role as Security Adviser." **The Washington Post,** (4 Aug. 1976), sec. B, p. 1, col. 1.

1359 Peterson, I. "Computer Hacking and Security Costs." **Science News,** 124, no. 19 (5 Nov. 1983), p. 294.

1360 _____. "Faster Factoring for Cracking Computer Security." **Science News,** 125, no. 2 (14 Jan. 1984), p. 20.

1361 _____. "New Data Increase Computer Crime Concerns." **Science News,** 125, no. 25 (23 June 1984), p. 390.

1362 Peterson, Ivars. "Computer Crime: Insecurity in Numbers."
Science News, 122, no. 1 (3 July 1982), pp. 12-14.

1363 _____. "Substance, Shadow and Computer Storage."
Science News, 121, no. 21 (22 May 1982), p. 346.

1364 _____. "Whom Do You Trust?" **Science News,** 120, no.
13 (26 Sept. 1981), pp. 205-6.

1365 Petras, Dorothy Donahue, and Susan Scarpelli. "Computers, Medical Malpractice, and the Ghost of the T.J.
Hooper." **Rutgers Journal of Computers and the Law,**
5, no. 1 (1975), pp. 15-49.

1366 "Petty Patents in the Federal Republic of Germany: A
Solution to the Problem of Computer Software Protection?" **Southwestern University Law Review,** 8 (1976),
pp. 888-909.

1367 Pfeifer, Michael R. "Legal Protection of Computer Software: An Update." **Orange County Bar Journal,** 5, no. 3
(Fall 1978), pp. 226-47.

1368 Pierce, Kay H. "Copyright Protection for Computer Programs." **Copyright Law Symposium,** 30 (1983), pp. 1-32.

1369 Plishner, Michael J. "'It's None of Your Business.' Or Is It?
California Addresses the Computer Age." **Rutgers Journal of Computers, Technology and the Law,** 8, no. 2
(1981), pp. 235-66.

1370 Ploman, Edward W. "Transborder Data Flows: The International Legal Framework." **Computer/Law Journal,** 3
(Summer 1982), pp. 551-62.

1371 "The Policy Implications of Granting Patent Protection to
Computer Software: An Economic Analysis." **Vanderbilt Law Review,** 37, no. 1 (Jan. 1984), pp. 147-81.

1372 Pomerance, Drew. "Case Digest." **Computer/Law Journal,**
2, no. 3 (Summer 1980), pp. 777-85.

1373 Pooley, James. "Trade Secrets." **Computerworld,** 16, no. 12 (22 Mar. 1982), pp. ID 1-3, 5-6, 10, 12+.

1374 Pope, Michael Alan, and Patrick Bruce Pope. "Protection of Proprietary Interests in Computer Software." **Alabama Law Review,** 30, no. 3 (Spring 1979), pp. 527-60.

1375 Popper, H.R. "Technology and Programming—Is It a Problem in Definitions?" **APLA Quarterly Journal,** 5, no. 1 (1977), pp. 13-29.

1376 Porter, Janet. "Software Piracy Spurs Industry Action in UK." **Journal of Commerce,** 36 (22 Aug. 1984), sec. A, p. 4., col. 2.

1377 Porter, W. Thomas, Jr. "Computer Raped by Telephone... and Other Futuristic Felonies by Electronic Con Men Who Leave No Footprints." **The New York Times Magazine** (8 Sept. 1974), pp. 32-34, 36+.

1378 "Possible Improper Use of Fed's Computer Is Investigated." **The New York Times,** 132 (11 Dec. 1982), p. 47.

1379 "Pranksters Gain Access, Destroy Programs." **Computerworld,** 16, no. 6 (8 Feb. 1982), p. 49.

1380 "Pranksters, Pirates and Pen Pals." **Time,** 119, no. 18 (3 May 1982), p. 54.

1381 Prasinos, Nicholas. "Legal Protection of Software via Copyright." **APLA Quarterly Journal,** 8, no. 1 (1980), pp. 252-72.

1382 _____. "Worldwide Protection of Computer Programs by Copyright." **Publishing, Entertainment, Advertising and Allied Fields Law Quarterly,** 13, no. 3 (Winter 1975), pp. 323-51.

1383 _____. "Worldwide Protection of Computer Programs by Copyright." **Rutgers Journal of Computers and the Law,** 4, no. 1 (1974), pp. 42-85.

1384 "President Signs EFT Privacy Legislation." **EDPACS,** 6, no. 6 (Dec. 1978), pp. 13-14.

1385 "Preventing 'War Games'." **Newsweek,** 102, no. 10 (5 Sept. 1983), p. 48.

1386 "Prevention Years Away as Computer Crime Increases." **Electronics,** 46, no. 15 (19 July 1973), pp. 33-34.

1387 "Privacy Act of 1974: An Overview and Critique." **Washington University Law Quarterly,** 1976, no. 4 (Fall 1976), pp. 667-718.

1388 "Privacy and the Computer." **Accountant,** 175 (8 July 1976), pp. 36+.

1389 "Privacy Called No. 1 EFT Issue." **Electronic News,** 21 (20 Sept. 1976), p. 34.

1390 "Privacy, Computerized Information Systems, and Common Law—A Comparative Study in the Private Sector." **Gonzaga Law Review,** 18, no. 3 (1982-83), pp. 567-604.

1391 "Privacy, Law Enforcement, and Public Interest: Computerized Criminal Records." **Montana Law Review,** 36, no. 1 (Winter 1975), pp. 60-79.

1392 "Privacy Protection Study Commission Recommends Legislation." **Computer Law and Tax Report,** 4, no. 2 (Sept. 1977), pp. 3-4.

1393 "Privacy vs. the Public's Right to Know." **Computer Law and Tax Report,** 4, no. 8 (Mar. 1978), pp. 2-3.

1394 "Privacy vs. the Public's Right to Know." **Computer Law and Tax Report,** 5, no. 11 (June 1979), pp. 5-6.

1395 "A Program Called Pilfer." **The New York Times,** 130 (26 July 1981), p. F4.

1396 "Proposed Computer-Crime Legislation to Stiffen Penalties for Violators." **EDN,** 29 (17 May 1984), p. 303.

1397 "Protecting Proprietary Software." **Mini-Micro Systems,** 11, no. 7 (Aug. 1978), pp. 78-79.

1398 "Protecting the Agency from Computer Theft and Fraud." **Best's Review Life/Health Insurance Edition,** 83, no. 2 (June 1982), pp. 60+.

1399 "Protecting the Computer Environment." **Infosystems,** 29, no. 1 (Jan. 1982), pp. 64+.

1400 "Protecting the Data Cookie Jar." **Infosystems,** 28, no. 8 (Aug. 1981), pp. 36-38, 40.

1401 "Protecting Your Privacy." **Businessweek,** no. 2477 (4 Apr. 1977), pp. 103-6, 108.

1402 "Protection of Computer Programs: Resurrection of the Standard." **Notre Dame Lawyer,** 50, no. 2 (Dec. 1974), pp. 333-45.

1403 "Protection of Computer Software—A Hard Problem." **Drake Law Review,** 26, no. 1 (1976-77), pp. 180-98.

1404 "Protection of Privacy of Computerized Records in the National Crime Information Center." **University of Michigan Journal of Law Reform,** 7, no. 3 (Spring 1974), pp. 594-614.

1405 "The Protection of Property Rights in Computer Software." **Akron Law Review,** 14, no. 1 (Summer 1980), pp. 85-102.

1406 "The Protection of Property Rights in Computer Software." **Publishing, Entertainment, Advertising and Allied Fields Law Quarterly,** 19 (1980/81), pp. 265-87.

1407 "Protection of Proprietary Rights in Computer Programs: A 'Basic' Formula for Debugging the System." **St. John's Law Review,** 57, no. 1 (Fall 1982), pp. 92-126.

1408 Proxmire, William. "Out with the Garbage." **Trial,** 7, no. 2 (Mar.-Apr. 1971), pp. 18-19.

1409 "The Push-Button Criminals of the 80's." **U.S. News and World Report,** 89, no. 12 (22 Sept. 1980), pp. 39-40.

1410 "Questions Raised About Security of NBS Encryption Algorithm." **Computer Law and Tax Report,** 4, no. 2 (Sept. 1977), pp. 1-2.

1411 Quisumbing, Leonardo A. "Transnational Law and Computer Technology: Some Legal Problems and Humane Considerations." **Philippine Law Journal,** 53 (Mar. 1978), pp. 67-72.

1412 Rabin, Sander Marc. "Computerized Marketing and Com-
     petition: Some Antitrust Considerations." **Rutgers
     Journal of Computers and the Law,** 4, no. 2 (1975), pp.
     407-19.

1413 Ramey, Daniel. "Patentability of Software and Firmware."
     Patent and Trademark Review, 78, no. 3 (Mar. 1980),
     pp. 99-121.

1414 Randall, Robert. "Computer Fraud: A Growing Problem."
     Management Accounting, 59, no. 10 (Apr. 1978), pp.
     61-64.

1415 Ranii, David. "Computer Laws Add Up; Do They Go Far
     Enough?" **National Law Journal,** 6, no. 34 (30 Apr. 1984),
     p. 1, col. 2.

1416 _____. "High-Tech Prosecution Has Perils." **National
     Law Journal,** 6, no. 34 (30 Apr. 1984), p. 37, col. 1.

1417 Raysman, Richard. "Conflict Resolution." **Computerworld,**
     15, no. 39 (28 Sept. 1981), pp. ID 29-31.

1418 _____. "Of Computers and the Law." **The New York
     Times,** 129 (14 Sept. 1980), p. F18.

1419 _____. "Protection of Proprietary Software in the Com-
     puter Industry: Trade Secrets as an Effective Method."
     Jurimetrics Journal, 18, no. 4 (Summer 1978), pp. 335-
     51.

1420 _____. "Warranty Disclaimer in the Data Processing
     Contract." **Rutgers Journal of Computers and the Law,**
     6, no. 2 (1978), pp. 265-76.

1421 _____, and Peter Brown. "Claims of Fraud and Misrepre-
     sentation." **New York Law Journal,** 187, no. 62 (1 Apr.
     1982), p. 1, col. 1.

1422 _____, and _____. "Evolving Statutes on Computer
     Crime." **New York Law Journal,** 189, no. 7 (11 Jan. 1983),
     pp. 1-2.

1423 Reaves, Lynne. "The Chips Police: 30 Hunt Silicon Valley
     Thieves." **American Bar Association Journal,** 69 (July
     1983), p. 884.

1424 Reed, Richard C. "Suit Alleging Illegal Tie-In Between Banking and Data Processing." **Computers and People**, 27, no. 3 (Mar. 1978), pp. 26, 18.

1425 "Reference Service Suggests Ways to Protect DP." **Computerworld**, 15, no. 41 (12 Oct. 1981), p. 34.

1426 Reider, Harry R. "Safeguarding Computer Records." **The CPA Journal**, 43, no. 1 (Jan. 1973), pp. 63-66.

1427 "Report to Cover Regulatory, Legal DP Issues." **Computerworld**, 15, no. 45 (9 Nov. 1981), p. 69.

1428 "Researchers Say Security Kernal Posing Obstacle." **Computerworld**, 17, no. 19 (9 May 1983), p. 25.

1429 Reznick, Allan E. "Synercom Technology, Inc. v. University Computing Co.: Copyright Protection for Computer Formats and the Idea/Expression Dichotomy." **Rutgers Journal of Computers, Technology and the Law**, 8, no. 1 (1980), pp. 65-84.

1430 Rhodes, Wayne L. "Computer Crime Is No Crime at All." **Infosystems**, 26, no. 8 (Aug. 1979), pp. 50, 52.

1431 Ribicoff, Abraham. "Introduction." **Computer/Law Journal**, 2, no. 2 (Spring 1980), pp. xvii-xviii.

1432 "Right of Privacy." **Trial**, 7, no. 2 (Mar.-Apr. 1971), p. 13.

1433 Riley, Tom. "Data Protection Today and Some Trends." **Law/Technology**, 17, no. 1 (1st Quarter 1984), pp. 3-12.

1434 "Risk Assessment for Distributed Systems." **EDP Analyzer**, 18, no. 4 (Apr. 1980), pp. 1-13.

1435 Rittenberg, Larry E., and Gordon B. Davis. "The Roles of Internal and External Auditors in Auditing EDP Systems." **The Journal of Accountancy**, 144, no. 6 (Dec. 1977), pp. 51-58.

1436 Rivlin, Gary. "A Multi-Million Dollar Crime Has Just Been Committed in This Room." **Student Lawyer**, 10, no. 6 (Feb. 1982), pp. 14-18, 35-36.

1437 "Roaming Hi-Tech Pirates." **Time,** 119, no. 6 (8 Feb. 1982), p. 61.

1438 Roberts, John G. "Cash Dispensers Trap Criminals." **Burroughs Clearing House,** 59, no. 1 (Oct. 1974), pp. 46,48,50.

1439 Roberts, John T. "The Current Law of Patents for Computer Software: Or Benson Revisited." **Computer/Law Journal,** 1, no. 1 (Spring 1978), pp. 85-104.

1440 Robertson, Wyndham. "Those Daring Young Con-Men of Equity Funding." **Fortune,** 88, no. 2 (Aug. 1973), pp. 81-85+.

1441 Robinson, James D. "Payments, People, Privacy: A Challenge of the Eighties." **Computers and People,** 29, nos. 7-8 (July-Aug. 1980), pp. 7-9, 22.

1442 Roddy, John. "The Federal Computer Systems Protection Act." **Rutgers Journal of Computers, Technology and the Law,** 7, no. 2 (Spring 1980), pp. 343-65.

1443 Rodgers, Gary L. "Auditors' Watchdog Role in Computer Fraud." **Commercial Law Journal,** 86, no. 5 (May 1981), pp. 173-78, 183.

1444 Rogers, Michael. "The Making of a Hacker." **Newsweek,** 102 (5 Sept. 1983), p. 44.

1445 Romney, Marshall. "Fraud and EDP." **The CPA Journal,** 46, no. 11 (Nov. 1976), pp. 23-28.

1446 Romney, Marshall B., and Jack L. Krogstad. "Management Accountants—In the Middle of the Computer Muddle." **Cost and Management,** 52, no. 3 (May-June 1978), pp. 4-9.

1447 Rooms, Peter L.P., and John Dexter. "Problems of Data Protection Law for Private Multinational Communication Networks." **Computer Networks,** 3, no. 3 (June 1979), pp. 205-14.

1448 Root, Joseph E., III. "Protecting Computer Software in the '80s: Practical Guidelines for Evolving Needs." **Rutgers Journal of Computers, Technology and the Law,** 8, no. 2 (1981), pp. 205-34.

1449 Rose, Alan C. "Protection of Intellectual Property Rights in Computers and Computer Programs: Recent Developments." **Pepperdine Law Review,** 9 (1982), pp. 547-67.

1450 Rosenbaum, Joseph I. "Software Piracy: Formulating a Plan for Protection." **Computerworld,** 17, no. 37 (12 Sept. 1983), pp. 149-154.

1451 Rosenberg, Ronald. "Why the Judge Cited DEC for Fraud." **Mini-Micro Systems,** 11, no. 5 (June 1978), pp. 14, 17.

1452 Ross, Otho B., III. "The Patentability of Computer 'Firmware'." **Journal of the Patent Office Society,** 59, no. 12 (Dec. 1977), pp. 731-78.

1453 _____. "The Patentability of Software and Firmware." **Computer Law Service,** 3, §4-2, art. 5 (1978), pp. 1-20.

1454 Rule, James B. "Electronic Funds Transfer and Federal Privacy Policy." **Jurimetrics Journal,** 18, no. 1 (Fall 1977), pp. 56-79.

1455 "Rules for Export of Hardware to Communist Countries Revised." **Computer Law and Tax Report,** 3, no. 12 (July 1977), pp. 2-3.

1456 Sadatoshi, Suzuki. "Computer Catches Kidnapper." **FBI Law Enforcement Bulletin,** 44, no. 6 (June 1975), pp. 14-18.

1457 "Safety Si, Rules No Says EFTS Report." **Computer Decisions,** 10, no. 1 (Jan. 1978), p. 11.

1458 "Salcris System Protects Against Software Piracy." **Computerworld,** 16, no. 7 (15 Feb. 1982), p. 51.

1459 Saltzer, Jerome H. "Ongoing Research and Development on Information Protection." **ACM Operating Systems Review,** 8, no. 3 (July 1974), pp. 8-24.

1460 Salzman, Alan E. "International Protection for Computer Software." **Law and Computer Technology,** 12, no. 1 (1st Quarter 1979), pp. 3-28.

1461 Samuels, Jeffrey M., and Linda B. Samuels. "The Patentability of Computer-Related Inventions." **The Corporation Law Review,** 6, no. 1 (Winter 1983), pp. 144-55.

1462 Scafetta, Joseph, Jr. "Computer Software and Unfair Methods of Competition." **The John Marshall Journal of Practice and Procedure,** 10, no. 3 (Spring 1977), pp. 447-64.

1463 _____. "Computer Software Protection: The Copyright Revision Bills and Alternatives." **The John Marshall Journal of Practice and Procedure,** 8, no. 3 (Spring 1975), pp. 381-99.

1464 _____. "Programming Technology as an Infringement." **APLA Quarterly Journal,** 5, no. 1 (1977), pp. 35-48.

1465 Scaletta, Phillip J. "Privacy Rights and Electronic Funds Transfer Systems—an Overview." **Catholic University Law Review,** 25, no. 4 (Summer 1976), pp. 801-11.

1466 Scannell, Tim. "Apple Computer to Remove Software Protection." **Computerworld,** 15, no. 43 (26 Oct. 1981), p. 13.

1467 _____. "Burroughs Found Guilty in B700 Suit." **Computerworld,** 16, no. 14 (5 Apr. 1982), pp. 1, 8.

1468 _____. "Burroughs Must Pay $250,000 to B700 User." **Computerworld,** 15, no. 28 (13 July 1981), pp. 1, 4.

1469 _____. "Burroughs to Appeal Verdicts in Fraud Suits." **Computerworld,** 15, no. 29 (20 July 1981), p. 7.

1470 _____. "Guilty Verdict for Burroughs in B800 Case." **Computerworld,** 16, no. 18 (3 May 1982), pp. 1, 8.

1471 _____. "Jury Finds for Burroughs in First Trial Involving B800." **Computerworld,** 15, no. 34 (24 Aug. 1981), pp. 1, 10.

1472 _____. "Massachusetts Drafts Computer Crime Bill." **Computerworld,** 15, no. 51 (21 Dec. 1981), p. 8.

1473 _____. "Most Firms' DP Centers Seen Vulnerable to Abuse Despite Safeguards, Laws." **Computerworld,** 15, no. 45 (9 Nov. 1981), pp. 23-24.

1474 _____. "Vendor's Papers Open to User." **Computerworld,** 15, no. 28 (13 July 1981), pp. 1, 6.

1475 Schjølberg, Stein. "Computer-Assisted Crime in Scandinavia." **Computer/Law Journal,** 2, no. 2 (Spring 1980), pp. 457-69.

1476 Schlesinger, Robert N. "Case Digest." **Computer/Law Journal,** 1, no. 3 (Winter 1979), pp. 573-609.

1477 Schmidt, Dan. "Fighting the War Against EDP Crime." **Management Today** (Dec. 1981), pp. 89-90, 92, 95.

1478 Schmidt, Walter E. "Legal Proprietary Interests in Computer Programs: The American Experience." **Jurimetrics Journal,** 21, no. 4 (Summer 1981), pp. 345-404.

1479 "School Invites Hackers to Break Into Its Systems." **Computerworld,** 17, no. 40 (3 Oct. 1983), p. 13.

1480 Schultz, Brad. "AI Projects Cloaked in Security." **Computerworld,** 15, no. 38 (21 Sept. 1981), p. 12.

1481 _____. "Expert Gives Strong Advice to Halt DP Abuse." **Computerworld,** 15, no. 39 (28 Sept. 1981), p. 14.

1482 _____. "Expert Warns DP Standards Could Endanger Legal Cases." **Computerworld,** 15, no. 46 (16 Nov. 1981), p. 31.

1483 _____. "Panelists 'Debate' Censorship of Cryptology." **Computerworld,** 16, no. 24 (14 June 1982), p. 27.

1484 _____. "Prof: Success of MIS Depends on Firm's Politics." **Computerworld,** 15, no. 28 (13 July 1981), p. 30.

1485 _____. "Should Research Be Censored for Security." **Computerworld,** 16, no. 19 (10 May 1982), p. 26.

1486 _____. "Structured Analysis Said to Cut Security Risks." **Computerworld,** 16, no. 20 (17 May 1982), p. 24.

1487 _____. "Would Certification Ensure 'Moral' DP Staff?" **Computerworld,** 15, no. 38 (21 Sept. 1981), p. 11.

1488 Schwartz, Lloyd. "House Passes Bill to Fight Computer, Credit Card Crime." **Electronic News,** 30 (30 July 1984), p. 16, col. 4.

1489 Schwartz, Michael B. "Safeguarding EFT's." **Datamation,** 29, no. 2 (Feb. 1983), pp. 148+.

1490 Schwinger, Robert A. "Banking Law: III. Electronic Fund Transfers." **Annual Survey of American Law,** 1983, no. 3 (Feb. 1984), pp. 770-76.

1491 Scoma, L., Jr. "Computer Security." **Office,** 78 (Aug. 1973), pp. 48-49.

1492 "Secrecy Order Lifted." **Science News,** 114, no. 1 (1 July 1978), p. 7.

1493 "Security Device Introduced for Data Base Protection." **Computerworld,** 16, no. 48 (29 Nov. 1982), pp. 77.

1494 "Security Legislation Seen on Upswing." **Computerworld,** 15, no. 33 (17 Aug. 1981), p. 14.

1495 "Security Levels Added to Version of Testing Package for NCR Users." **Computerworld,** 16, no. 38 (20 Sept. 1982), p. 40.

1496 "Security of Source Document." **Data System** (Aug. 1977), pp. 10-11.

1497 "Security Package Guards Against Data Piracy." **Computerworld,** 16, no. 25 (21 June 1982), p. 39.

1498 "Security Package Unveiled." **Computerworld,** 16, no. 21 (24 May 1982), p. 50.

1499 "Security Steps Guard Against Computer Fraud." **Automation,** 20, no. 7 (July 1973), p. 14.

1500 "Security Updated for CICS Site." **Computerworld,** 15, no. 25 (22 June 1981), p. 29.

1501 "'Security/3000' Protects HP Users." **Computerworld,** 15, no. 28 (13 July 1981), p. 55.

1502 Seipel, Peter. "Teledoc and Open Records." **Computer/Law Journal,** 3 (Summer 1982), pp. 457-513.

1503 Selinger, Jerry R. "Protecting Computer Software in the Business Environment: Patents, Copyrights and Trade

Secrets." **The Journal of Law and Commerce,** 3 (1983), pp. 65-90.

1504 _____. "Protection of Proprietary Software: Evolving Needs for Legal Protection in the Modern-Day Business." **Texas Bar Journal,** 45, no. 1 (Jan. 1982), pp. 11-19.

1505 "Senate Bill Would Help Federal Attorneys Fight Computer Crime." **Office,** 89 (Mar. 1979), p. 76.

1506 Shankar, K.S. "The Total Computer Security Problem: An Overview." **Computer,** 10, no. 6 (June 1977), pp. 50-62, 71-73.

1507 Shannon, Daniel. "Copycatting in the Software Patch." **The New York Times,** 131 (9 May 1982), p. F17, col. 1.

1508 Sheehan, John, and Jerrold Thompson. "Bank Records v. Privacy: Is There a Viable Solution." **Glendale Law Review,** 3 (1978-79), pp. 235-48.

1509 Sheridan, James A. "Patent Protection of Computer Software—Practical Insights." **Santa Clara Law Review,** 23, no. 4 (1983), pp. 989-99.

1510 Shick, Blair C. "Privacy—The Next Big Issue in EFT." **Banking,** 68, no. 3 (March 1976), pp. 70, 72, 74, 76.

1511 Shickich, Joseph E., Jr. "Transborder Data Flow." **Law and Computer Technology,** 11, no. 3 (3rd Qtr 1978), pp. 62-74.

1512 Shields, Hannah, and Mae Churchill. "Criminal Data Banks: The Fraudulent War on Crime." **The Nation,** 219, no. 21 (21 Dec. 1974), pp. 648-55.

1513 Shoor, Rita. "Software Commission Targets Key Issues." **Computerworld,** 15, no. 41 (12 Oct. 1981), p. 11.

1514 "Short-Circuiting Computer Crime." **Pit and Quarry,** 74 (Dec. 1981), p. 91.

1515 "Short Circuiting the Crooks." **Forbes,** 126, no. 9 (27 Oct. 1980), p. 72.

1516 "Should There Be a Corporate Right of Privacy?" **Computer Law and Tax Report,** 5, no. 1 (Aug. 1978), p. 5.

1517 Sills, Arthur J. "Automated Data Processing and the Issue of Privacy." **Seton Hall Law Review,** 1, no. 1 (Spring 1970), pp. 7-24.

1518 Simkin, M.G. "Is Computer Crime Important?" **Journal of Systems Management,** 33 (May 1982), pp. 34-38.

1519 Simkin, Mark G. "Computer Crime: Lessons and Direction." **The CPA Journal,** 51, no. 12 (Dec. 1981), pp. 10, 12-14.

1520 Simpson, Christopher. "Consultant Convicted in Trade Secrets Theft." **Computerworld,** 15, no. 29 (20 July 1981), p. 15.

1521 _____. "Electronics Underworld: Feds Cap Smugglers' Pipeline Stretching from Silicon Valley to Soviet Union." **Computerworld,** 15, no. 35 (31 Aug. 1981), pp. 1, 6-7, 9.

1522 _____. "High Tech Smugglers: 60% of Those Caught Try Again." **Computerworld,** 15, no. 37 (14 Sept. 1981), pp. 1, 8.

1523 _____. "How Can You Protect Yourself from Smugglers." **Computerworld,** 15, no. 37 (14 Sept. 1981), pp. 81-82.

1524 _____. "Trail of Stolen Intel Chips Leads to Siemens." **Computerworld,** 15, no. 36 (7 Sept. 1981), pp. 1, 8-10.

1525 "Simultaneous Copyright and Trade Secret Protection for Computer Programs." **Santa Clara Law Review,** 23, no. 4 (1983), pp. 1037-63.

1526 Singel, John B., Jr., and O. Bruce Gupton, Jr. "Privacy Regulations Are Coming." **Price Waterhouse Review,** 21, no. 1 (1976), pp. 11-18.

1527 Singer, Ted. "DP Hackers Not Our Greatest Threat." **Computerworld,** 17, no. 46 (14 Nov. 1983), p. 84.

1528 Sittenfeld, Linda R. "Toward International Regulation of the Transfer of Technology?" **Law/Technology,** 14, no. 3 (3rd Quarter 1981), pp. 2-17.

1529 Skelly, Stephen J. "Balancing Privacy and Efficiency in an Electronic World." **Law and Computer Technology,** 12, no. 2 (2nd Quarter 1979), pp. 38-49.

1530 Skillern, Frank L., Jr. "Recent Developments Under the Bankers Blanket Bond." **The Forum,** 17 (Summer 1982), pp. 1282-90.

1531 Skrine, Bruce E. "A Primer in Electronic Fund Transfers." **Law Notes for the General Practitioner,** 16, no. 4 (Fall 1980), pp. 97-101.

1532 Slappey, Sterling G. "A Lot of People Know Your Secrets." **The Nation's Business,** 62, no. 10 (Oct. 1974), pp. 30-34.

1533 Slivka, R.T., and J.W. Darrow. "Methods and Problems in Computer Security." **Rutgers Journal of Computers and the Law,** 5, no. 2 (1976), pp. 217-69.

1534 Smith, Larry W. "A Survey of Current Legal Issues Arising from Contracts for Computer Goods and Services." **Computer/Law Journal,** 1, no. 3 (Winter 1979), pp. 475-99.

1535 Smith, Richard H., and E. Robert Yoches. "Legal Protection of Software via Trade Secrets." **APLA Quarterly Journal,** 8, no. 1 (1980), pp. 240-51.

1536 "So Far, 18 State Computer Crime Laws." **Computerworld,** 17, no. 13 (28 Mar. 1983), p. 6.

1537 "Software Copyright: Government Tells How to Do It." **Computer Law and Tax Report,** 4, no. 7 (Feb. 1978), pp. 3-4.

1538 "Software: Copyright, Trade Secret or Patent?" **Computerworld,** 15, no. 48 (30 Nov. 1981), p. 24.

1539 "Software Patent Issue Is Murky." **The New York Times,** 128 (28 June 1978), p. D6, col. 2.

1540 "Software Piracy and the Personal Computer: Is the 1980 Software Copyright Act Effective?" **Computer/Law Journal,** 4, no. 1 (Summer 1983), pp. 171-93.

1541 "Software Protection Group Seeking New Membership." **Computerworld,** 15, no. 50 (14 Dec. 1981), p. 36.

1542 "Software Protection: Patents, Copyrights, and Trade Secrets." **Albany Law Review,** 35, no. 4 (1971), pp. 695-717.

1543 "Software Rental, Piracy, and Copyright Protection."
Computer/Law Journal, 5, no. 1 (Summer 1984), pp. 125-
41.

1544 "Software Rentals: Piracy Is the Hot New Issue." **Business
Week,** no. 2801 (1 Aug. 1983), pp. 90-91.

1545 "Software Should Be Patentable." **Computers and People,**
24, no. 12 (Dec. 1975), pp. 14-16.

1546 Sokolik, Stanley L. "Computer Crime—The Need for Deterrent Legislation." **Computer/Law Journal,** 2, no. 2
(Spring 1980), pp. 353-83.

1547 Soltysinski, Stanislaw J. "Computer Programs and Patent
Law: A Comparative Study." **Rutgers Journal of Computers and the Law,** 3, no. 1 (1973), pp. 1-82.

1548 Soma, John T., and Richard A. Wehmhoefer. "A Legal and
Technical Assessment of the Effect of Computers on
Privacy." **Denver Law Journal,** 60, no. 3 (1982), pp. 449-
83.

1549 _____, Rodney D. Peterson, Gary Alexander, and Curt
W. Petty. "The Communications Regulatory Environ-
ment in the 1980's." **Computer/Law Journal,** 4, no. 1
(Summer 1983), pp. 1-54.

1550 "Some Early Thoughts on the Wells Fargo Case." **ABA
Banking Journal,** 73, no. 7 (July 1981), p. 57.

1551 "Sophisticated Crime." **Dun's Review,** 114, no. 2 (Aug.
1979), pp. 88, 90, 94.

1552 Spanner, Robert A. "Who Owns Innovation?" **Computerworld,** 16, no. 38 (20 Sept. 1982), pp. ID 33-38, 40.

1553 _____. "Who Owns Innovation?" **Computerworld,** 16, no.
39 (27 Sept. 1982), pp. 43-44, 46-53.

1554 Spindle, L. "Computer Security." **Radio-Electronics,** 55
(Feb. 1984), p. 111.

1555 "Spotting the Computer Crook." **Science Digest,** 74, no. 4
(Oct. 1973), p. 39.

1556 "The Spreading Danger of Computer Crime." **Business Week**, no. 2684 (20 Apr. 1981), pp. 86-92.

1557 Sprowl, James A. "Proprietary Rights in Programmed Computers: Looking Beyond the Hardware/Software Distinction for More Meaningful Ways of Characterizing Proprietary Interests in Digital Logic Systems." **Arizona State Law Journal**, 1983, no. 4 (1983), pp. 611-784.

1558 _____. "A Review of Niblett's Legal Protection of Computer Programs and Diamond v. Diehr and Some Thoughts on Patenting Computer Programs." **American Bar Foundation Research Journal**, 1981, no. 2 (Spring 1981), pp. 559-69.

1559 Squires, Jeffrey. "Copyright and Compilations in the Computer Era: Old Wine in New Bottles." **Bulletin of the Copyright Society of the U.S.A.**, 24, no. 1 (Oct. 1976), pp. 18-46.

1560 Srinivasan, Cadambi, and Paul E. Dascher. "Computer Security and Integrity: Problems and Prospects." **Infosystems**, 28, no. 5, part 1 (May 1981), pp. 116, 118, 121-123.

1561 Stadlen, Godfrey. "Survey of National Data Protection Legislation." **Computer Networks**, 3, no. 3 (June 1979), pp. 174-86.

1562 "Stand-Alone Security Device Out." **Computerworld**, 17, no. 16 (18 Apr. 1983), p. 72.

1563 Station, James E. "Standard Contracts for Users a Poor Idea." **Computerworld**, 15, no. 41 (12 Oct. 1981), pp. 71,74.

1564 "The Status of Patent Law Concerning Computer Programs: The Proper Form for Legal Protection." **Drake Law Review**, 33, no. 1 (1983-1984), pp. 155-75.

1565 Steinberg, Stephen R. "Disputes Over Computer Software Warranties." **National Law Journal**, 5, no. 32 (18 Apr. 1983), p. 15, col. 3.

1566 Steinmuller, Wilhelm. "Legal Problems of Computer Networks: A Methodological Survey." **Computer Networks**, 3, no. 3 (June 1979), pp. 187-98.

1567 "Stemming the Tide of Video Game Piracy: Copyright Protection for the Audiovisual Displays." **Brooklyn Law Review,** 49, no. 4 (Summer 1983), pp. 889-909.

1568 Stern. "Security for Your Computer Facility." **Office,** 58 (Aug. 1978), p. 18.

1569 Stern, Richard H. "Another Look at Copyright Protection of Software: Did the 1980 Act Do Anything for Object Code?" **Computer/Law Journal,** 3 (Fall 1981), pp. 1-17.

1570 Stevens, George E., and Harold M. Hoffman. "Tort Liability for Defamation by Computer." **Rutgers Journal of Computers and the Law,** 6, no. 1 (1977), pp. 91-102.

1571 Stone, Jack. "Concern Mounting Over Data Controls for Credit Reporting Agencies." **Computerworld,** 17, no. 31 (1 Aug. 1983), p. 29.

1572 _____. "How to Foul Up a System Without Even Trying." **Computerworld,** 15, no. 51 (21 Dec. 1981), p. 35.

1573 _____. "Human Connection—Big Board Serves as Model for DP Security." **Computerworld,** 17, no. 30 (25 July 1983), p. 47.

1574 Stone, Robert. "Some Security and Integrity Controls in Small Computer Systems." **Journal of Accountancy,** 141, no. 2 (Feb. 1976), pp. 36, 38, 40.

1575 Stone, Robert L. "Who Is Responsible for Computer Fraud?" **Journal of Accountancy,** 139, no. 2 (Feb. 1975), pp. 35-39.

1576 Stork, Philip. "Legal Protection for Computer Programs: A Practicing Attorney's Approach." **ASCAP Copyright Law Symposium,** 20, (1972), pp. 112-39.

1577 Stout, Donald E. "Protection of Programming in the Aftermath of Diamond v. Diehr." **Computer/Law Journal,** 4, no. 2 (Fall 1983), pp. 207-42.

1578 Streeter, Bill. "People, More Than Technology, Are Still Key to EFT Security." **ABA Banking Journal,** 74, no. 7 (July 1982), pp. 29, 33-34, 37.

1579 "Strict Products Liability and Computer Software: Caveat Vendor." **Computer/Law Journal,** 4, no. 2 (Fall 1983), pp. 373-400.

1580 Strother, Robert S. "Crime by Computer." **Reader's Digest,** 108, no. 648 (Apr. 1976), pp. 143-44, 146-48.

1581 "Students Abuse Computers for the Challenge." **Computerworld,** 16, no. 21 (24 May 1982), p. 8.

1582 Sugarman, Robert. "On Foiling Computer Crime." **IEEE Spectrum,** 16, no. 7 (July 1979), pp. 31-32.

1583 "A Suggested Legislative Approach to the Problem of Computer Crime." **Washington and Lee Law Review,** 38, no. 4 (Fall 1981), pp. 1173-94.

1584 Sumner, John P. "Computer Software Protection..." **Bench & Bar of Minnesota,** 41, no. 3 (Mar. 1984), pp. 15-17.

1585 "Supreme Court Agrees to Rule on Patentability of Computer Programs." **BNA's Patent, Trademark & Copyright Journal,** no. 66 (24 Feb. 1972), pp. A12-A13.

1586 "Supreme Court Called Upon Again to Determine Fate of Computer Programs." **BNA's Patent, Trademark & Copyright Journal,** no. 354 (17 Nov. 1977), pp. A1-A2.

1587 "Supreme Court Called Upon to Overturn Rulings That Claims Employing Computer Programs Are Patentable." **BNA's Patent, Trademark & Copyright Journal,** no. 329 (19 May 1977), pp. A1-A2.

1588 "Supreme Court Declares Computer Program Unpatentable: Action by Congress Needed." **BNA's Patent, Trademark & Copyright Journal,** no. 104 (23 Nov. 1972), p. A1.

1589 "Supreme Court Denies Flook a Patent." **Computer Law and Tax Report,** 5, no. 1 (Aug. 1978), pp. 1-2.

1590 "Supreme Court Is Called Upon to Prevent 'Circumvention' of Gottschalk v. Benson." **BNA's Patent, Trademark & Copyright Journal,** no. 217 (27 Feb. 1975), pp. A9-A13.

1591 "Supreme Court Still Ducks Decision on Software Patents; CCPA Confuses Problem." **Computer Law and Tax Report,** 4, no. 5 (Dec. 1977), p. 6.

1592 "Supreme Court to Review Patent Cases." **Computer Law and Tax Report,** 6, no. 10 (May 1980), p. 2.

1593 "Supreme Court Will Take Another Look at Patentability of Computer Programs." **BNA's Patent, Trademark & Copyright Journal,** no. 228 (15 May 1975), p. Al.

1594 Swanson, C.R., and Leonard Territo. "Computer Crime: Dimensions, Types, Causes, and Investigation." **Journal of Police Science and Administration,** 8, no. 3 (Sept. 1980), pp. 304-11.

1595 "Sweden Regulates Those Snooping Data Banks." **Business Week,** no. 2300 (6 Oct. 1973), pp. 93, 95.

1596 Sykes, D.J. "Protecting Data by Encryption." **Datamation,** 22 (Aug. 1976), pp. 81+.

1597 "System Capacity Fizzles; Bottler Sues Consultant." **Computerworld,** 15, no. 33 (17 Aug. 1981), p. 25.

1598 Taber, John K. "On Computer Crime (Senate Bill S.240)." **Computer/Law Journal,** 1, no. 3 (Winter 1979), pp. 517-43.

1599 _____. "A Survey of Computer Crime Studies." **Computer/Law Journal,** 2, no. 2 (Spring 1980), pp. 275-327.

1600 Taffer, Lewis M. "The Making of the Electronic Fund Transfer Act: A Look at Consumer Liability and Error Resolution." **University of San Francisco Law Review,** 13, no. 2 (Winter 1979), pp. 231-44.

1601 Tangorra, Joanne. "The Fight Against Software Piracy: Lotus Founder Defines a Plan." **Publishers Weekly,** 226, no. 8 (24 Aug. 1984), pp. 34-35, 40.

1602 Taylor, Alan. "What's Going On with the VA and Mumps?" **Computerworld,** 15, no. 29 (20 July 1981), pp. 33, 35.

1603 "Telephone Company's Investigation of Computer Bandit OK Under Title III." **The Criminal Law Reporter,** 24, no. 15 (17 Jan. 1979), pp. 2308-9.

1604 Tell, Larry. "Firms Face Computer Theft Issue." **The National Law Journal,** 4, no. 24 (22 Feb. 1982), pp. 1, 28-29.

1605 "Theft by Computer: Small Is Big." **Colorado Business,** 9 (May 1982), p. 59.

1606 "Theft of Computer Time." **EDPACS,** 5, no. 12 (June 1978), p. 7.

1607 "This Is What You Thought About Cash Machines, Plastic Money and Computer Crime." **Glamour,** 82 (Feb. 1984), p. 35.

1608 Thompson, Seymour F. "The Invasion of Privacy and Electronic Fund Transfer Systems: Spotlight on the Invaders." **Computers and People,** 25, no. 9 (Sept. 1976), pp. 12-13.

1609 Thorne, Jack F. "Control of Computer Abuses." **Journal of Accountancy,** 138, no. 2 (Oct. 1974), pp. 40, 42, 44, 46.

1610 Thornton, Barbara. "White v. State of California and Penal Code Sections 11120-11127: A Pre-Computer Privacy Case and the Legislative 'Answer'." **The Los Angeles Bar Bulletin,** 47, no. 9 (July 1972), pp. 320-30, 356-64.

1611 "Those Little Words Mean What They Say." **Computer Law and Tax Report,** 4, no. 1 (Aug. 1977), pp. 1-3.

1612 "Those Little Words Mean What They Say—Exactly." **Computer Law and Tax Report,** 4, no. 11 (June 1978), pp. 1-2.

1613 " 'Top Secret' Security Tool Updated." **Computerworld,** 16, no. 51 (20 Dec. 1982), p. 33.

1614 "Trade Secret Protection of Computer Software." **Computer/Law Journal,** 5, no. 1 (Summer 1984), pp. 77-99.

1615 "Trade Secrets and the Skilled Employee in the Computer Industry." **Washington University Law Quarterly,** 61, no. 3 (1983), pp. 823-47.

1616 "Trade Secrets Have Problems Too." **Computer Law and Tax Report,** 6, no. 2 (Sept. 1979), pp. 6-7.

1617 "Transborder Data Flows: Personal Data-Recommendations of the Organisation for Economic Co-Operation and Development Concerning Guidelines Governing the Protection of Privacy and Transborder Flows of Personal Data, O.E.C.D. Doc. C(80)58 (Oct. 1, 1980)." **Harvard International Law Journal**, 22, no. 1 (Winter 1981), pp. 241-47.

1618 "Transnational Data Regulation: A Computer-Generated Problem." **Computer Law and Tax Report**, 4, no. 6 (Jan. 1978), pp. 3, 6-7.

1619 Troy, Gene. "Thwarting the Hackers." **Datamation**, 30, no. 10 (1 July 1984), pp. 116-18, 122-23, 126, 128.

1620 "Trying to Solve the Product Liability Mess." **Computer Law and Tax Report**, 5, no. 7 (Feb. 1979), pp. 4-7.

1621 Tunick, David C. "Computer Law: An Overview." **Loyola of Los Angeles Law Review**, 13, no. 2 (Mar. 1980), pp. 315-51.

1622 Turn, Rein. "Privacy Protection and Security in Business Computer Systems." **Atlanta Economic Review**, 26, no. 6 (Nov.-Dec. 1976), pp. 24-30.

1623 _____, and W.H. Ware. "Privacy and Security in Computer Systems." **American Scientist**, 63, no. 2 (Mar.-Apr. 1975), pp. 196-203.

1624 "Two Arrested in Chip Heist from Monolithic." **Computerworld**, 16, no. 10 (8 Mar. 1982), p. 7.

1625 "Two OPM Principles Plead Guilty to Fraud Charges." **Computerworld**, 16, no. 12 (22 Mar. 1982), p. 77.

1626 Ubell, Franklin D. "Electronic Funds Transfer and Antitrust Laws." **The Banking Law Journal**, 93, no. 1 (Jan. 1976), pp. 43-81.

1627 Ulmer, Eugen. "Copyright Protection of Software Works with Special Reference to Computer Programs." **International Review of Industrial Property and Copyright Law**, 2, no. 1 (1971), pp. 56-70.

1628 "The Ultimate Heist." **Time**, 112, no. 21 (20 Nov. 1978), p. 48.

1629 "Unauthorized Use of Government Computer Can Be Theft." **Computer Law and Tax Report,** 4, no. 10 (May 1978), pp. 1-2.

1630 "University Will Fight Research Secrecy Order." **Science News,** 113, no. 23 (10 June 1978), p. 373.

1631 "Unlocking the Potential in Electronic Keys." **Business Week,** no. 2676 (23 Feb. 1981), p. 107.

1632 Upchurch, Gregory E. "A Template for Judicial Resolution of Computer Program Patentability." **Georgia Law Review,** 9, no. 4 (Summer 1975), pp. 855-91.

1633 "Use and Abuse of Computerized Information: Striking a Balance Between Personal Privacy Interests and Organizational Information Needs." **Albany Law Review,** 44, no. 3 (Apr. 1980), pp. 589-619.

1634 "User Suit Against Honeywell Awaits Ruling." **Computerworld,** 17, no. 44 (31 Oct. 1983), p. 13.

1635 "Using Computer Time No Crime, Judge Says." **American Bar Association Journal,** 68 (June 1982), p. 671.

1636 "Using Computers to Steal—Latest Twist in Crime." **U.S. News and World Report,** 74, no. 25 (18 June 1973), pp. 39-40, 42.

1637 "Validating the Source Code: How One Vendor Does It." **Computer Law and Tax Report,** 6, no. 7 (Feb. 1980), pp. 4-5.

1638 "Vendor Convicted for Violating Client's Security." **EDPACS,** 5, no. 12 (June 1978), p. 8.

1639 "Ven-Tel Files Suit Against Former Workers." **Computerworld,** 15, no. 37 (14 Sept. 1981), p. 85.

1640 Visserman, Peter, and John C. Moran. "Legal Protection of Computer Software." **Illinois Bar Journal,** 71, no. 10 (June 1983), pp. 608-12.

1641 _____, and _____. "Legal Protection of Computer Software." **Patent and Trademark Review,** 81, no. 11 (Nov. 1983), pp. 457-66.

1642 Vogel, Peter S. "Law and Computers: Current Issues."
Texas Bar Journal, 43, no. 8 (Sept. 1980), pp. 757-65.

1643 Volgyes, Mary R. "The Investigation, Prosecution, and
Prevention of Computer Crime: A State-of-the-Art
Review." **Computer/Law Journal**, 2, no. 2 (Spring 1980),
pp. 385-402.

1644 Voris, J. Walker. "How the Computer Can Be Used to
Commit Fraud." **The Practical Accountant**, 8, no. 2
(Mar.-Apr. 1975), pp. 63-64.

1645 "WIPO: Legal Protection of Computer Software." **Journal
of World Trade Law**, 17, no. 6 (Nov.-Dec. 1983), pp. 537-
45.

1646 Walker, Barry. "Theft by Computer—The Invisible Crime."
Journal of Insurance, 42, no. 2 (Mar.-Apr.1981), pp. 30-4.

1647 Walker, Craig M. "Computer and High Technology Product Liability in the 1980s." **The Forum**, 19 (Summer 1983),
pp. 684-93.

1648 _____. "Computer Litigation and the Manufacturer's
Defenses Against Fraud." **Computer/Law Journal**, 3
(Spring 1982), pp. 427-55.

1649 "Wanted: Computers That Will Not Compute for Criminals." **Nation's Business**, 66, no. 11 (Nov. 1978), p. 38.

1650 "The Warranty of Merchantability and Computer Software
Contracts: A Square Peg Won't Fit in a Round Hole."
Washington Law Review, 59, no. 3 (July 1984), pp. 511-31.

1651 Washburn, Pat. "Electronic Journalism, Computers and
Privacy." **Computer/Law Journal**, 3 (Winter 1982), pp.
189-209.

1652 Watkins, Peter. "Computer Crime: Separating the Myth
from the Reality." **CA Magazine**, 114, no. 1 (Jan. 1981),
pp. 44-47.

1653 Watson, Bruce L. "Disclosure of Computerized Health
Care Information: Provider Privacy Rights Under Supply
Side Competition." **American Journal of Law & Medi-
cine**, 7, no. 3 (Fall 1981), pp. 265-300.

1654 Weaver, Warren, Jr. "High Court Denies Computer Patent for Programming." **The New York Times**, 122 (21 Nov. 1972), p. 1, col. 5.

1655 Weber, Ron. "An Audit Perspective of Operating System Security." **Journal of Accountancy**, 140, no. 3 (Sept. 1975), pp. 97-100.

1656 Weinstein, David. "Confidentiality of Criminal Records— Privacy v. The Public Interest." **Villanova Law Review**, 22, no. 6 (Oct. 1977), pp. 1205-13.

1657 Weiss, H. "Computer Security: An Overview." **Datamation**, 20 (Jan. 1974), pp. 42-47.

1658 Wessel, Milton R. "Some Implications of the Software Decision." **Jurimetrics Journal**, 14, no. 2 (Winter 1973), pp. 110-12.

1659 "What Do You Know About Computer and White-Collar Crime?" **Drug Topics**, (6 Apr. 1979), p. 59.

1660 "What's Wrong with Punitive Damages?" **Computer Law and Tax Report**, 5, no. 9 (Apr. 1979), pp. 1-2.

1661 "When IRS Computers Dig into Your Tax Return." **U.S. News and World Report**, 84, no. 14 (10 Apr. 1978), pp. 49-50.

1662 "When Thieves Sit Down at Computers." **U.S. News and World Report**, 96, no. 25 (25 June 1984), p. 8.

1663 "Where Do We Stand on Computer Crime Laws?" **Computer Law and Tax Report**, 6, no. 6 (Jan. 1980), pp. 3-5.

1664 "Where the Computer Criminal Can Have a Field-Day." **Data Systems**, 1978 (Mar. 1978), pp. 24-25.

1665 "White Collar Crime: A Survey of the Law: Computer Crime." **American Criminal Law Review**, 18, no. 2 (Fall 1980), pp. 370-86.

1666 "White Collar Crime: Second Annual Survey of the Law— II. Substantive Crimes—Computer Crime." **American Criminal Law Review**, 19, no. 1 (Fall 1981), pp. 499-509.

1667 "White Collar Crime: Second Annual Survey of the Law—II. Substantive Crimes—Mail and Wire Fraud." **American Criminal Law Review**, 19, no. 1 (Fall 1981), pp. 287-95.

1668 "White House Still Deciding on Direction." **Computerworld**, 16/17, nos. 52/1 (27 Dec. 1982/3 Jan. 1983), p. 64.

1669 White, J.V. "Privacy in the Information Society." **Vital Speeches of the Day**, 48, no. 10 (1 Mar. 1982), pp. 313-15.

1670 White, Travis Gordon. "Trademark Protection of Computer Software." **APLA Quarterly Journal**, 8, no. 3 (1980), pp. 279-93.

1671 Whitebook, Joan Sharon, and Umberto Tosi. "Protecting Computerland's Fragile New Trade Secrets." **California Lawyer**, 2, no. 9 (Oct. 1982), pp. 43-47.

1672 Whiteside, Thomas. "Annals of Crime. Dead Souls in the Computer—I." **The New Yorker**, 53, no. 27 (22 Aug. 1977), pp. 35-38, 40+.

1673 _____. "Annals of Crime. Deal Souls in the Computer—II." **The New Yorker**, 53, no. 28 (29 Aug. 1977), pp. 34-36, 38+.

1674 "Who Cooked the Computer?" **Time**, 99, no. 9 (1 Mar. 1982), p. 61.

1675 "Why Isn't There a Standard Computer Contract?" **Computer Law and Tax Report**, 3, no. 10 (May 1977), pp. 3-4.

1676 "Why the Acceptance Provisions in the Contract Are So Important." **Computer Law and Tax Report**, 6, no. 9 (Apr. 1980), pp. 1-3.

1677 Wicklein, John. "How Sweden Keeps Its Computers Honest." **The Progressive**, 44, no. 11 (Nov. 1980), pp. 34-38.

1678 Wiegner, Kathleen K. "Pirates Versus Piranhas." **Forbes**, 132, no. 4 (15 Aug. 1983), pp. 35-36.

1679 Williams, Elaine. "Scotland Yard and Home Office in an All-Out Effort to Fight Crime by Computer." **The Engineer**, 246, no. 6363 (9 Mar. 1978), pp. 12-13.

1680 "Williams Electronics, Inc. v. Artic International, Inc.: Duplication of Computer Program in Object Form Is Copyright Infringement." **South Texas Law Journal**, 24, no. 1 (1983), pp. 399-420.

1681 Willis, Donald S. "Who Knows You: A Look at Commercial Data Banks." **Computers and Automation**, 22, no. 3 (Mar. 1973), pp. 18-21.

1682 Wilson, Norman L., Jr. "Game War in the Courts: 'Munchkin' vs. Pac-Man." **Computerworld**, 16, no. 32 (9 Aug. 1982), pp. 37-38.

1683 _____. "When Is Software Patentable? Some Signs Exist." **Computerworld**, 16, no. 35 (30 Aug. 1982), pp. 76, 81.

1684 _____. "Who Owns Inventions? Employees or Employers?" **Computerworld**, 17, no. 25 (20 June 1983), pp. 53-54.

1685 Winkler, Ronald L. "The National Commission on Electronic Fund Transfers: Problems and Prospects." **Washington University Law Quarterly**, 1977, no. 3 (1977), pp. 507-12.

1686 Wirbel, Loring. "Somebody Is Listening." **The Progressive**, 44, no. 11 (Nov. 1980), pp. 16-19, 21-22.

1687 Wolfson, Douglas K. "From the Legislature: An Overview of the Report of the National Commission on Electronic Fund Transfer Systems." **Rutgers Journal of Computers and the Law**, 6, no. 1 (1977), pp. 103-11.

1688 Wood, Helen M. "The Use of Passwords for Controlling Access to Remote Computer Systems and Services." **National Computer Conference**, 46 (1977), pp. 27-33.

1689 Wood, Stephen G. "Computers and the Protection of Individual Liberties." **The American Journal of Comparative Law**, 30 (1982), pp. 583-600.

1690 Woodcock, Virgil E. "Mental Steps and Computer Programs." **Journal of the Patent Office Society**, 52, no. 5 (May 1970), pp. 275-92.

1691 "World Intellectual Property Organization Advisory Group: A Report." **Law and Computer Technology,** 7, no. 5 (Sept.-Oct. 1974), pp. 124-38.

1692 "World-Wide Protection of Computer Software: An Analysis of the WIPO Draft Proposals." **New York Law School Journal of International and Comparative Law,** 2, no. 2 (1981), pp. 278-315.

1693 Wormser, David A. "Licensing Laws May Get Tougher." **Computerworld,** 17, no. 17 (25 Apr. 1983), pp. ID 1-6, 8-9.

1694 Wurst, Harold E. "Patents on Computer Programs." **Los Angeles Bar Bulletin,** 46, no. 6 (Apr. 1971), pp. 213-16, 219.

1695 Wyden, R. "Curbing the Keyboard Criminal." **USA Today,** 112 (Jan. 1984), pp. 68-70.

1696 Yogodzinski, Debra. "Electronic Funds Transfer Systems—An Analysis of Federal and State Criminal Law." **Commerical Law Journal,** 83, no. 6 (June-July 1978), pp. 276-87.

1697 Zalud, Bill. "Computer Criminals Will Be Prosecuted: Adopting a 'Prevention First' Attitude." **Data Management,** 21, no. 4 (Apr. 1983), pp. 30-31, 45.

1698 Zammit, Joseph P. "Computers, Software, and the Law." **American Bar Association Journal,** 68 (Aug. 1982), pp. 970-72.

1699 _____. "Contracting for Computer Products." **Jurimetrics Journal,** 22, no. 3 (Spring 1982), pp. 337-54.

1700 Zientara, Marguerite. "Bankruptcy Blamed on 13-Year Fraud via DP." **Computerworld,** 16, no. 43 (25 Oct. 1982), p. 6.

1701 _____. "Colleges Fear Higher Degree of DP Abuse: Tighter Security Evolving." **Computerworld,** 16, no. 21 (24 May 1982), pp. 1, 8.

1702 _____. "Embezzler Volunteers to Redesign Victim's System." **Computerworld,** 17, no. 26 (27 June 1983), p. 4.

1703 _____. "FAA Takes Steps to Prevent Possible Sabotage." **Computerworld,** 15, no. 32 (10 Aug. 1981), p. 7.

1704 _____. "Two DPers Caught in Ariz." **Computerworld,**
17, no. 28 (11 July 1983), p. 14.

Coauthor Index

Subject Index

Reagan 1084, 1093-1098, 1100
Records--See Credit Records; Criminal Justice Records; Em-
    ployment Records; Medical Records; Personal Records--
    General; Taxpayer Records
Regulation E 86, 87, 748; See Also Electronic Fund Transfer Act
Rhode Island 322
Ribicoff 296
Right to Financial Privacy Act of 1978 779
Risk Analysis/Management 154, 155, 193, 290, 780, 925, 1434,
    1486
S.240--See Federal Computer Systems Protection Act (of 1977
    or 1979)
S.898 906, 907
S.1201--See Semiconductor Chip Protection Act of 1983
S.1766--See Federal Computer Systems Protection Act (of 1977
    or 1979)
S.1920--See Small Business Computer Crime Prevention Act
S.2065--See Electronic Fund Transfer Consumer Protection Act
Sabotage 625, 942, 956, 1009, 1484, 1703
Salami Techniques 50, 1342
Scandinavia 1475
Scavenging 50
Secret Service 258, 1099
Security and Security Measures 1, 3, 12, 17, 25, 26, 28, 29, 33,
    35, 37, 39, 41, 45, 48, 64-69, 75, 78, 79, 83, 88, 90, 91, 94,
    105-107, 109, 111, 113, 114, 117, 118, 122-127, 130, 132-136, 139,
    140, 141, 145, 150, 152-155, 159-162, 168, 175, 176, 178, 181-184,
    186, 189, 191-195, 205, 207, 208, 210, 211, 214, 216, 217, 219,
    221-223, 229, 238, 239, 242-244, 251-254, 265, 267, 269,
    272, 274, 275, 277, 279-281, 283, 291-293, 300, 318, 319,
    342, 374, 377, 380, 382-384, 408, 424, 436, 441, 443, 444,
    446, 465, 473, 479, 488, 492, 511, 512, 535-538, 544, 556,
    561, 562, 568, 581, 586, 588, 608, 614, 616, 626-629, 639,
    649, 668, 669, 671, 672, 677, 685, 686, 695, 696, 698, 705,
    710, 715, 780, 781, 788, 808, 810, 821, 838, 854, 860, 871,
    872, 881, 882, 886, 887, 899, 901, 923, 924, 933, 934, 937,
    938, 945, 947, 949, 964, 975, 984, 990, 991, 994, 1000-1002,
    1008, 1011, 1012, 1033, 1035, 1036, 1055, 1066, 1071, 1083, 1084,
    1086, 1087, 1094, 1110, 1120, 1161, 1164, 1168, 1169, 1171, 1172,
    1177, 1191, 1198, 1200, 1209, 1210, 1212, 1222, 1234, 1236, 1237,
    1239, 1240, 1256, 1270, 1279, 1280, 1295, 1300, 1301, 1306,
    1338, 1345, 1348, 1353, 1356, 1358-1360, 1363, 1364, 1385,
    1386, 1395, 1410, 1425, 1426, 1428, 1433, 1434, 1446, 1451,
    1458, 1459, 1477, 1480, 1486, 1487, 1491-1501, 1506, 1514, 1515,
    1523, 1533, 1554-1556, 1560, 1562, 1568, 1571, 1572-1574,